IMAGES
of America

EARLY POVERTY ROW STUDIOS

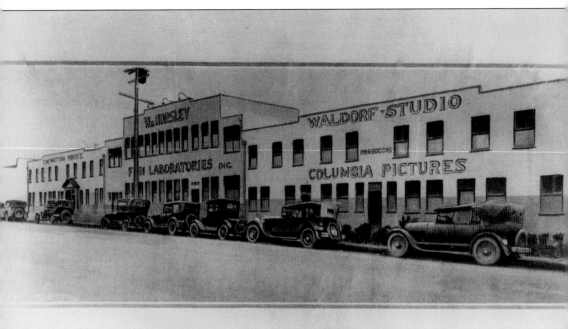

Poverty Row

Poverty Row is the land of the free producers, home of the brave-hearted, the independents, the states righters, the little 'uns

POVERTY ROW STUDIOS, 1925. Rather than avoid the disparaging nickname "Poverty Row," early producers chose to embrace it, as is evident from this 1925 advertisement, which proclaims that "Poverty Row is the land of the free producers, home of the brave-hearted, the independents, the states righters, the little 'uns." Depicted in this drawing are, from left to right, C.W. Patton Productions at 6050 Sunset Boulevard, the William Horsley Laboratory at 6060 Sunset Boulevard, and the Waldorf Studio at 6070 Sunset Boulevard. Waldorf was the birthplace of Columbia Pictures, proving that sometimes the "little 'uns" got big. (Courtesy Bison Archives.)

ON THE COVER: MONOGRAM PICTURES, 1941. One of Poverty Row's best-known tenants was Monogram Pictures, created in the early 1930s through the merger of Trem Carr's Sono Art–World Wide Pictures and W. Ray Johnston's Rayart Productions. Monogram was famous for its low-budget Westerns and for the "Monogram Nine," a collection of horror films starring Bela Lugosi. For two years in the mid-1930s, Monogram was part of Herbert Yates's Republic Pictures before again going independent. (Courtesy Bison Archives.)

IMAGES
of America

EARLY POVERTY ROW STUDIOS

E.J. Stephens and Marc Wanamaker

ARCADIA
PUBLISHING

Published by Arcadia Publishing
Charleston, South Carolina

Printed in the United States of America

Library of Congress Control Number: 2014941231

For all general information, please contact Arcadia Publishing:
Telephone 843-853-2070
Fax 843-853-0044
E-mail sales@arcadiapublishing.com
For customer service and orders:
Toll-Free 1-888-313-2665

Visit us on the Internet at www.arcadiapublishing.com

Dedicated to the thousands of early cinematic pioneers,
who took a chance and changed the world

CONTENTS

ACKNOWLEDGMENTS

The authors would like to thank everyone at Arcadia Publishing for their hard work, especially our editor Jared Nelson.

E.J. would like to thank Marc Wanamaker for his passion, his encyclopedic knowledge of early Hollywood, and his priceless Bison Archives collection. He would also like to thank his good friend Steve Goldstein, who, along with Theodore Hovey of Hollywood Forever Cemetery, helped him right an old wrong by finally getting Ford Sterling's crypt marked. But mostly, he thanks his beautiful wife, editor, and soul mate, Kimi, who reminds him with every glance that he is the luckiest man alive.

Marc Wanamaker would like to thank E.J. Stephens for helping him put this book together and for his excellent writing skills. He would like to thank his late mother, Edith Wanamaker, for helping him catalogue his collections over the years (before computers), organizing voluminous amounts of information culled from countless sources.

Thanks also go to Robert S. Birchard for the use of photographs and for his research on early motion picture companies. Major thanks to Hollywood Heritage, who helped preserve the Lasky-DeMille Studio Barn. Thanks to the Academy of Motion Picture Arts and Sciences for its Margaret Herrick Research Library. Others who contributed to the photographic research and information include Michael Peter Yakaitis, Tommy Ryan, Mike Hawks, Linda Mehr, Matt Seversen, Cecilia DeMille Presley and Helen Cohen of the Cecil B. DeMille Estate, Kevin Brownlow, George Pratt (formerly of the Eastman House), Ray Stuart, Larry Edmunds Bookshop, Howard Mandelbaum of Photofest in New York, Movie Star News, UCLA Archives, USC Archives, American Film Institute Library, University of Madison Wisconsin, Georgetown University Archives, Andy Lee of the Universal Research Library, Jimmy Earie of the MGM Research Library, Lillian Michelson of the Goldwyn Research Library, Ken Kenyon of the 20th Century Fox Research Department, Kellum DeForest of the RKO Research Library, Fred Jorden of Producers Studio, the Rosenthal family of Raleigh Studios, Bill Kenly of Paramount Publicity in New York, Jack Warner Jr., Universal Old Timers Club, Hal Roach, Brent Christo, Dick Bann, British Film Institute Archives, Bruce Torrence, Dino and Greg Williams, Jesse Lasky Jr., Cinemabilia of New York, Collectors Bookshop in Hollywood, Mary Corliss of the MOMA in New York, John Kobal, and many others. All information and photographs are courtesy of Bison Archives.

INTRODUCTION

In the first decade of the 20th century, Hollywood was still miles from the encroaching city of Los Angeles, cattle herds ambled down unpaved Sunset Boulevard, and the marketing of demon liquor was strictly verboten.

It was at this time that the first wave of West Coast cinematic pioneers stepped into this obscure hamlet, where initially film crews were as unwelcome as blight on the vineyards bordering Vine Street.

Many settled around the intersection of Sunset Boulevard and Gower Street at an area that came to be known as "Poverty Row." It was here, before the rise of the major studios, that an industry of light and movement secured its first toehold in Hollywood.

During this era, Poverty Row was a catch-as-catch-can kind of place, where most producers lived from film to film, feasting or failing based on the take from hundreds of nickelodeon tills scattered throughout the country. Most of these start-ups folded or were absorbed by larger concerns, but a few, namely Warner Bros. (WB) and Columbia, took root, prospered, and are still with us today.

But for every WB or Columbia, there were dozens of other production houses that came and went along Poverty Row, with names like L-KO Motion Picture Company, Amalgamated, Russell Productions, Century Film Corp., Christie Studios, Harry Joe Brown, Crown, Norman Dawn, Goodman, Goodwill, Granada, Hutchison, Morante, Ben Wilson, Kinemart, Phil Goldstone, Bud Barsky, Bischoff/California, Big Chief, Color Craft, Charles J. Davis, Gold Medal, Pacific Pictures, and Yaconelli Productions, to name just a few.

Over time, Hollywood became more of a conceptual term than a geographic one, as most of the "Hollywood" movies made throughout history came from studios located in places like Burbank, Glendale, and the film "cities"—Studio City, Culver City, Century City, and Universal City.

The same can be said for Poverty Row, which was stretched to include producers from other places around Los Angeles whose own struggle to hang on to the "Hollywood" landscape was often a story more intriguing than the plots of the serialized cliffhangers that many produced.

In the early 20th century, Hollywood was much like dozens of other rural hamlets sprinkled throughout Southern California, known for its mild Mediterranean climate, ample agriculture, varied vistas, and 350 days of sunshine a year. It was a snobby town, unfriendly towards film people and their creations.

The area had been Mexican territory just a few decades earlier until the treaty that led to it becoming American soil was signed in 1847 at what is today the entrance to Universal Studios. The future film capital was a rich agricultural area 40 years later when teetotaler Harvey Wilcox and his young bride, Daeida, purchased a 160-acre parcel of farmland with the intention of subdividing it for residents of their planned temperance community.

The region was well known at the time for its figs, citrus, melons, avocados, and grapes, but two products that it did not produce in abundance were holly, which would not take to the soil, and wood, since the land was unforested and covered by chaparral. The genesis of the name came during a train trip Daeida Wilcox took where a female passenger told her about a summer home she owned named Hollywood back in the eastern part of the United States. Liking the name, Wilcox penned it to the new settlement, forever linking the name of an unknown vacation home with the mythical industry of image.

Today, the name Hollywood is so synonymous with the film industry that it is assumed that the choice to center the motion picture business here was an inevitable one. This was certainly not the case. How the movie industry got here is more a story of happy accidents rather than careful planning.

The community created by the Wilcoxes officially incorporated in 1903 as a 24-square-mile city with about 1,500 residents. Ironically, as future events would play out, the new town prohibited the sale of liquor. In another ironic twist, this ban on booze may have been the chief contributing factor for the film industry first sprouting here.

The city's incorporation, and its prohibition on alcohol, had knocked Rene Blondeau and his popular tavern out of business. To recoup his investment, and possibly to poke the ribs of the snootier members of the citizenry, his widow (Rene died in 1903) rented out the building at the northwest corner of Sunset Boulevard and Gower Street to the only thing the residents hated more that liquor—"movies," as film people, and not their creations, were then called.

The Centaur Film Company of Bayonne, New Jersey, was the first tenant. Centaur's founders, the English brothers David and William Horsley, came west to find a suitable place to make films. Attracted by Hollywood's landscapes, sunlight, and cheap labor, the Horsleys rented the former tavern in 1911 for $40 a month. They were soon joined by filmmaker Al Christie, creating the Nestor Studio, Hollywood's first.

Other film studios moved into the area around Nestor, which by 1912 had been absorbed by the new Universal conglomeration of small, formerly independent producers. A year later, Universal opened its first Western studio across the street from Nestor. When Universal moved to new digs shortly afterwards, this studio housed the L-KO Motion Picture Company and the Stern Brothers Century Film Company.

By 1916, the area surrounding the former Blondeau Tavern was sprinkled with other upstart "studios," if the name can properly apply to the ramshackle hovels that most of these concerns inhabited. The two-city-block area bordered by Sunset Boulevard on the north, Gordon Street on the east, Fountain Avenue to the south, and Gower Street on the west quickly filled with fly-by-night production companies, earning itself the "Poverty Row" nickname. It quickly became a hangout for directors, cameramen, film cutters, technicians, and actors vying for jobs. The corner of Sunset Boulevard and Gower Street took on the added sobriquet of "Gower Gulch" after a fight broke out between two cinema cowboys looking for work, which culminated with one man's death.

Many of the Poverty Row producers appeared and quickly disappeared. Others with names like Horsley, Christie, Balshofer, Lehrman, and Bischoff kept popping up throughout the history of early Hollywood.

It was common for Poverty Row producers to partner together to gain a firmer financial footing in the industry. Some of these mergers proved successful, like in the case of Trem Carr's Sono Art–World Wide Pictures and W. Ray Johnston's Rayart Productions, which joined forces in the early 1930s to become Monogram, a name still familiar to fans of Westerns and schlocky horror films. Monogram for a time became part of Republic Pictures, which was itself created by bringing several Poverty Row production houses together. Republic, which was headquartered in Studio City, operated successfully as a mini-major studio famous for its Gene Autry, Roy Rogers, and John Wayne films, among others.

The rapid changes taking place in their community did not sit well with many of its more conservative members, who disparaged the newcomers as provincial riff-raff, unfit to tread in their paradise-on-earth community. Community leaders, especially the former Daeida Wilcox (she married Philo Judson Beveridge after being widowed in 1891), cared little for the carryings-on of the film people. She collectively saw them as a group only interested in pushing social mores far past the limit of respectability, especially in the realm of drinking, which she detested.

Hollywood as an independent entity only lasted for seven years. Its growing population was rapidly exhausting the infant city's water supply, prompting the village to willingly give up its independence (and its prohibition on liquor) to become the latest conquest of the rapidly growing city of Los Angeles.

In August 1914, at the time armies in Europe were firing the first shots of World War I, Daeida Beveridge passed away after witnessing, to her horror, the transformation of her quaint, formerly dry community into the headquarters of America's film industry.

Why did the studios come to Hollywood?

It is an interesting question, as film's many birthplaces were all far away from Hollywood, in places like New York, Paris, northern New Jersey, Lyons, France, and a dozen other spots. America's first film center was in New York, where interiors were most likely filmed on rooftops, and location shooting was often carried out across the Hudson River in New Jersey. (1903's *The Great Train Robbery*, the first silent American Western blockbuster, was filmed in the wilds of Milltown, New Jersey.)

New York was a difficult place for early filmmakers to operate, especially during the winter, when an abundance of sunlight—the most important ingredient needed for early film stock—was scarce. This prompted many early producers to winter in more temperate climates, such as Florida and Cuba. Some chose to go to California, which, in addition to providing ample sunlight, offered cheap labor and varied landscapes for exterior shooting.

There was an added incentive for many to head westward. In 1908, American überinventor Thomas Edison created the Motion Pictures Patents Company (MPPC), which consisted of a conglomeration of several film companies (Edison, Biograph, Vitagraph, Essanay, Selig, Lubin, Kalem, Star Film Company, and American Pathé), the leading distributor, and film manufacturer Eastman Kodak. The MPPC, or Edison Trust as it came to be known, stifled entry into motion-picture making, as only members of the Trust were allowed to use Edison filming equipment or Kodak film. The MPPC regulated everything about filmmaking, including where movies could be shown and the length of films, initially limiting them to one reel (13–17 minutes).

Independent producers soon found Southern California to be a more desirable location than back East since it was more difficult for the MPPC to enforce its patents there. These new arrivals still had to keep vigilant when filming, as goons hired by the Trust would often show up and wreck productions not licensed by the MPPC.

By the time the Trust was declared unconstitutional by the US Supreme Court in 1915, these new imports had already established Southern California as America's new moviemaking headquarters.

Film crews first arrived in downtown Los Angeles as early as 1898, which is understandable, being that it was the largest metropolitan area in the region. But why did they venture six miles north to Hollywood a decade later?

There does not seem to be any single clear-cut answer. Sure, Hollywood had plenty of sunshine, but so did the rest of Southern California. The same was true for cheap labor. And the entire region was far from Edison and his Trust. Hollywood had varied vistas, but it did not have a coastline or a cityscape, something that nearby cities like Santa Barbara and San Diego could boast.

It is possible that Hollywood became synonymous with filmed entertainment due to a combination of the law of unintended consequences coupled with luck. As already mentioned, Hollywood's prohibition on liquor gave the district its first studio, against the wishes of its citizenry. But this enterprise, and its followers, may have all withered and died without making Hollywood a movie town had certain other happenings not played out during these early years.

One of these tipping points was the success of the 1914 Jesse L. Lasky Feature Play Company production *The Squaw Man*, which was one of if not the first full-length motion picture filmed by a Hollywood studio. Cecil B. DeMille, one of the film's directors, intended to make the movie in several Western states, but time constraints forced the company on to Los Angeles. While there, DeMille learned of a small barn/studio he could rent for cheap six miles to the north.

The Squaw Man proved so successful that it propelled Lasky up from the ranks of Poverty Row and into the upper echelon of the infant industry. It also turned the trickle of producers arriving in Hollywood into a torrent. Two years later, Lasky would expand his Hollywood footprint by merging with Adolph Zukor's Famous Players Film Company, creating what would become today's Paramount Pictures. From then on, there was no turning back. Hollywood had arrived for good.

The history of filmmaking in America could have been quite different had Daeida Wilcox Beveridge acquired a taste for ardent spirits or if Cecil B. DeMille had stepped off a train in, say, Santa Barbara and set up shop. Had either of these events occurred, the name "Hollywood" may have remained as anonymous as the summer home from which its moniker sprouted.

Travel with us a century into the past to a place disparagingly known as Poverty Row in the sparsely settled village of Hollywood, where creativity and energy, blended with hope, gave birth to the American home of an industry of movement and magic.

One

SOUTHERN CALIFORNIA'S
FIRST POVERTY ROW

In 1907, Chicago film producer Col. William Selig sent Francis Boggs and a unit of the Selig Polyscope Company to Los Angeles. Their mission was to set up a film studio in Southern California to take advantage of the region's plentiful sunshine. They initially settled on a rooftop of a building on Main Street near Eighth Street, where they shot scenes for *Monte Cristo*, a one-reel historical thriller.

Two years later, Selig sent Boggs to downtown Los Angeles to create an outdoor studio behind a Chinese laundry. Here, they made the first feature film on the West Coast, entitled *The Heart of a Race Tout*.

In 1910, Biograph sent its director-general D.W. Griffith to Los Angeles to set up a makeshift studio in a portion of a Pacific Electric trolley yard in downtown Los Angeles. That same year, Selig opened a studio in Los Angeles's Edendale district modeled after the San Gabriel Mission, which included a bell tower over the main gate.

Also in 1909, New York's Bison Film Company created a studio on a former horse ranch just south of the Selig Studio at 1712 Allesandro Street (now Glendale Boulevard). Bison's lot later became Mack Sennett's Keystone Film Company, the home of the Keystone Cops and the place from which Charlie Chaplin was introduced to the world.

Over the next several years, other studios opened in Edendale, including Norbig Studio, which began life as a rental lot and laboratory. For a time it was leased to Hal Roach of the Rolin Film Company and to Hobart Bosworth Productions, among others. The Reaguer Production Company occupied the same site from 1922 to 1924, when Westwood Productions took over. Nearby was the Pathé West Coast Studio at 1807 Allesandro Street.

Filmmaking had firmly taken root in Southern California by the early 1910s. Soon, producers would discover a place called Hollywood.

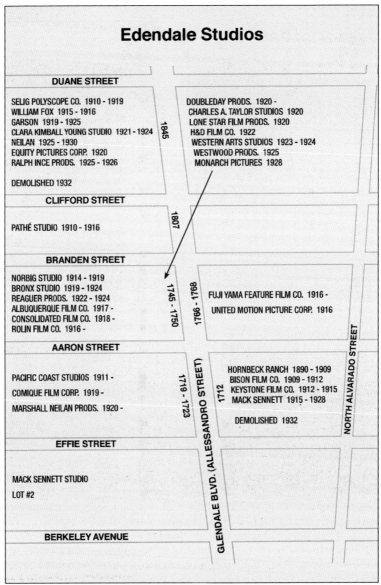

Edendale Studios

DUANE STREET

SELIG POLYSCOPE CO. 1910 - 1919
WILLIAM FOX 1915 - 1916
GARSON 1919 - 1925
CLARA KIMBALL YOUNG STUDIO 1921 - 1924
NEILAN 1925 - 1930
EQUITY PICTURES CORP. 1920
RALPH INCE PRODS. 1925 - 1926

DEMOLISHED 1932

DOUBLEDAY PRODS. 1920 -
CHARLES A. TAYLOR STUDIOS 1920
LONE STAR FILM PRODS. 1920
H&D FILM CO. 1922
WESTERN ARTS STUDIOS 1923 - 1924
WESTWOOD PRODS. 1925
MONARCH PICTURES 1928

1845

CLIFFORD STREET

PATHÉ STUDIO 1910 - 1916

1807

BRANDEN STREET

NORBIG STUDIO 1914 - 1919
BRONX STUDIO 1919 - 1924
REAGUER PRODS. 1922 - 1924
ALBUQUERQUE FILM CO. 1917 -
CONSOLIDATED FILM CO. 1918 -
ROLIN FILM CO. 1916 -

1745 - 1750

1766 - 1768

FUJI YAMA FEATURE FILM CO. 1916 -
UNITED MOTION PICTURE CORP. 1916

AARON STREET

PACIFIC COAST STUDIOS 1911 -

COMIQUE FILM CORP. 1919 -

MARSHALL NEILAN PRODS. 1920 -

1719 - 1723

GLENDALE BLVD. (ALLESSANDRO STREET)

1712

HORNBECK RANCH 1890 - 1909
BISON FILM CO. 1909 - 1912
KEYSTONE FILM CO. 1912 - 1915
MACK SENNETT 1915 - 1928

DEMOLISHED 1932

NORTH ALVARADO STREET

EFFIE STREET

MACK SENNETT STUDIO

LOT #2

BERKELEY AVENUE

GLENDALE BLVD. (ALLESSANDRO STREET)

EDENDALE MAP, 1910S. During the 1910s, the Los Angeles district of Edendale, located near Echo Park, was one of the biggest producers of motion pictures in the entire world. It was here that the first screen pie fight broke out. It was also here that Roscoe "Fatty" Arbuckle and Mabel Normand became household names. And it was also in Edendale that an unknown English music-hall performer named Charles Chaplin first picked up a cane and derby, pasted on a stage mustache, slid into some baggy pants and an unusually large pair of mismatched boots, and waddled into the hearts of movie watchers worldwide. The Edendale movie studios were concentrated in a four-block area of Allesandro Street (today's Glendale Boulevard), between Berkeley Avenue and Duane Street. Edendale was the first major moviemaking area of Southern California, but its fortunes proved fickle. Most of the studios left by the mid-1920s, and the memories of Edendale moviemaking—along with the name Edendale itself, which fell out of use—were soon forgotten. Today, all that is left of Keystone Studios, cinema's first great "laugh factory," is a stage that is now used as a commercial storage unit.

SELIG POLYSCOPE STUDIO, 1906 OR 1907. In 1907, Col. William Selig, a Chicago film producer, hired well-known stage director Francis Boggs to take a unit of his Selig Polyscope Company to the West Coast. They stopped briefly in Colorado before moving to California, where they constructed the first sets ever built in Los Angeles, pictured here, on a rooftop at the corner of Eighth and Olive Streets. Here they made a one-reel version of the opera *Carmen* and shot scenes for *Monte Cristo*, which had additional ocean scenes shot at Laguna Beach. Colonel Selig, nicknamed "The Man Who Invented Hollywood," was the first producer to take advantage of Southern California's varied vistas and ample sunlight. In the process, he put as much distance as he could between his company and Thomas Edison's stifling East Coast Film Trust, which he later reluctantly joined.

SELIG POLYSCOPE STUDIO, 1909. Colonel Selig again sent Francis Boggs on the road in 1909, along with a company of actors and cameraman James Crosby. Stopping first in New Orleans, they ended up in Los Angeles, where they set up "permanent facilities," pictured above and below, in the rear lot of the Sing Kee Chinese Laundry on Olive Street between Seventh and Eighth Streets. Above, cameraman James Crosby prepares to shoot a scene from *The Peasant Prince* while director Francis Boggs (in a white shirt with his back to the camera) offers instructions to his actors. Below, Boggs (third from left) prepares to shoot a scene for *The Heart of a Race Tout* at the Chinese Laundry lot.

SELIG POLYSCOPE COMPANY, 1914. In 1910, Colonel Selig opened one of the first studios in the Edendale area, located between southern Glendale and downtown Los Angeles, at 1845 Allesandro Street (now Glendale Boulevard). Colonel Selig was born during the Civil War and is one of the unheralded pioneers of Hollywood. Selig began performing in vaudeville while still a teenager. In 1896, he created his own film enterprise in Chicago, known as the Selig Polyscope Company, which was one of the first film companies in the United States. After moving west, Selig produced nearly 1,000 films and discovered Tom Mix. Selig's career was harmed by his belief that only short films would keep audiences drawn to theaters, causing him to miss out on the more lucrative feature-film market. His energy was further sapped when he was embroiled in a lawsuit claiming that Shakespeare's works were not in fact his own, fighting claims that the Bard's plays were written by Sir Francis Bacon—a rumor that has never completely been extinguished.

SELIG POLYSCOPE COMPANY, EDENDALE, 1910. Studio gatekeeper "St. Peter" Green (standing right) looks on as a Selig unit sets off for location filming through the Allesandro Street gate of the Selig Polyscope studio. Below, Francis Boggs (far left) directs while James Crosby turns the crank on the camera while filming *Girls of the Range* (1910). This stage, like most during this era, was open to the elements, thereby providing sufficient light to the early cinema equipment. Sunlight was a vital ingredient for early filming, and Southern California's advertised "350 days of sunshine" was a huge draw for filmmakers.

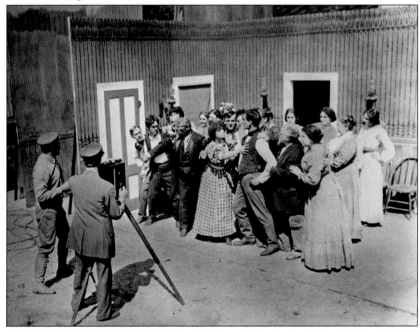

GARSON STUDIO, 1919. The former Selig Studio changed hands many times before being demolished in 1932. One of the owners was producer Harry Garson, who was partnered professionally and personally with film actress Clara Kimball Young. In the mid-1910s, Young was one of the most popular actresses of the silent era, rivaling even Mary Pickford and the Gish sisters. A much-publicized affair with Lewis J. Selznick harmed her career, and a later affair with Garson damaged it even further. Garson produced Young's films all around Hollywood prior to purchasing the old Selig lot. In 1925, Garson sold the studio to independent director Marshall Neilan, who began his film career while still in his teens when he got a job chauffeuring Biograph executives scouting sites for their new studio around Los Angeles. Presumably, Neilan took them to Edendale, where he owned his own studio a few years later. Neilan enjoyed a 45-year career in the motion picture business, not only as a producer but as an actor, screenwriter, and director as well.

BISON STUDIO, 1912. Around 1909, Fred Balshofer of the Bison Company, which was owned by the New York Motion Picture Company (NYMPC), came west and set up a studio at 1712 Allesandro Street (today's Glendale Boulevard) in Edendale to the south of Colonel Selig's lot. Balshofer later described Los Angeles during this time, remembering that they photographed scenes around the Echo Park and Hollywood areas, riding "their horses from the studio in Edendale to the hills of Hollywood over winding roads." The Bison crews used several vistas and ranches surrounding the studio for horse chases, gun battles, and stagecoach holdups. Balshofer soon discovered nearby Griffith Park, which he described as "a beautiful place with tree-covered hills, ideal for western pictures. It was only a few miles from our studio and many times we would set up an Indian village and leave it there for a few days at a time, in the section now known as the Griffith Park Golf Course." In the photograph, Adam Kessel (standing, center), vice president of NYMPC, supervises the rebuilding of the studio after it was transferred from Bison to Mark Sennett's Keystone Studios.

BISON STUDIO, 1909. The above photograph shows the cast of an unidentified Bison production, possibly *An Indian's Bride* (1909). Among the group are Native American actress Lillian St. Cyr (standing, far left), who performed under the name Princess Red Wing; producer Fred Balshofer (seated, far left); actor-producer Charles Bauman (seated, far right); and Native American actor James Young Deer (standing, far right). Charles Bauman helped create several film companies during his career, including Crescent, Bison, Keystone, New York Motion Picture, Broncho, Kay-Bee, Domino, Mutual, Kessel-Bauman, and Reliance. Red Wing, who later starred in the hit *The Squaw Man* (1914), was a full-blooded Sioux from the Ho-Chunk tribe of Nebraska. James Young Deer, her husband at the time, was from the Nanticoke tribe of Delaware. He was the first known person of Native American ancestry to ever direct a film. Below, the couple stands in front of some cinematic cowboys.

MACK SENNETT, 1914. Canadian-born "King of Comedy" Mack Sennett (standing, foreground) was the son of Irish Catholic immigrant farmers who moved to the United States when Sennett was still in his teens. The family was living in Northampton, Massachusetts, when Sennett decided to become a vaudevillian performer—a decision he later claimed Northampton mayor (and future US president) Calvin Coolidge tried to talk him out of. Sennett migrated to New York, where he became an actor and director for the Biograph Company. In 1912, Adam Kessel and Charles Bauman founded Keystone, which was placed at the former Bison lot at 1712 Allesandro Street (now Glendale Boulevard) in Edendale with Mack Sennett as head of production. Sennett soon introduced the Keystone Cops, the Mack Sennett Bathing Beauties, and Charlie Chaplin to the world. The roster of comedic talent that passed through the Keystone gates is staggering. In only a few short years, Charlie Chaplin, Mabel Normand, Ford Sterling, Roscoe "Fatty" Arbuckle, Harold Lloyd, Gloria Swanson, Louise Fazenda, Charley Chase, Ben Turpin, Marie Prevost, and Carole Lombard were all on the Keystone payroll.

KEYSTONE STUDIO, 1913.
Mack Sennett rebuilt Keystone Studios on the site of the former Bison lot, also incorporating an abandoned grocery store, a bungalow, which served as the administrative offices, and a barn the actors used as a dressing room. The original stage (which reads "Keystone Mack Sennett Keystone" in the photograph) still exists today as a rental storage unit.

KEYSTONE STUDIO, 1914. Pictured among this group are silent comedians Charles Murray (third from right), Mack Swain (second from right), and Polly Moran (far right), who all had long careers in film. Mack Swain had nearly 200 film credits but is best remembered today as Big Jim McKay, the starving prospector who shares a meal of a baked boot with Charlie Chaplin in *The Gold Rush* (1925).

CHARLIE CHAPLIN, 1914. Charlie Chaplin first stepped through the gates of the Keystone Studio at the age of 24 in December 1913. A seasoned veteran of the Fred Karno comedy troupe, Chaplin was unknown outside his native England. He left Keystone one year later as arguably the most famous man on earth. This photograph is believed to have been taken on Saturday, January 10, 1914, the day that Chaplin's most famous character, the Little Tramp, first appeared on screen. The film, *Kid Auto Races at Venice*, is a simple story of an actual soapbox derby that is being filmed by a camera crew, with Chaplin playing a "photo bomber" who keeps getting between the camera and the racers. In the photograph, cameraman Frank Williams stands behind the camera with Chaplin (center) and the film's director, Henry Lehrman, looking on. Chaplin left Keystone for more money at the end of 1914 after making 35 films. Sennett eventually moved the studio in 1928 to Studio City. He was forced to give it up five years later during the Great Depression.

NORBIG STUDIO, MID-1910s. Another early Edendale rental studio was named Norbig, pictured above in 1916, located at 1745 Allesandro Street (now Glendale Boulevard). Several of the biggest silent-screen comedians passed through Norbig on their way to other studio homes, including Hal Roach, who produced Harold Lloyd's *Lonesome Luke* films here, and Charlie Chaplin, who spent time here when he worked for Mutual. Incidentally, Mutual later built Chaplin his own studio at 1025 Lillian Way in Hollywood, which later became Buster Keaton Studios. Below is a shot of the filming at Norbig of 1914's *Burning Daylight*, which was made by actor-director Hobart Bosworth.

PATHÉ COMPANY OF AMERICA, 1911; REAGUER PRODUCTIONS, 1922. French-based Pathé Frères, one of the oldest film companies in the world, created a studio in Fort Lee, New Jersey, in 1914. That same year, it produced the outrageously successful serial *The Perils of Pauline*, starring Pearl White. At around the same time, Pathé hired Native American actor-director James Young Deer to make realistic Westerns at its new Pathé West Coast Studio at 1807 Allesandro Street (now Glendale Boulevard) in Edendale. Above is a photograph of the Pathé employees gathered together outside the studio. As director-general, Young Deer acted in, wrote, or directed over 150 films, mostly Westerns, which were noted (not surprisingly) for sympathetic portrayals of Native Americans. Below is a shot of Reaguer Productions, which was housed in the former Norbig Studios during 1922.

Two

HOLLYWOOD'S ORIGINAL POVERTY ROW

In Old California, the first film shot in Hollywood, was directed by none other than D.W. Griffith after he came west for the Biograph Company in 1910. Griffith photographed early Hollywood from the hills to the north, showing the sparsely settled landscape, dotted only by a sprinkling of buildings.

The first film lot in Hollywood was the Nestor Studio, owned by English brothers David and William Horsley of the Centaur Film Company of Bayonne, New Jersey. They sent a unit headed by directors Thomas Ricketts and Al Christie west in 1911. Ricketts made the *Desperate Desmond* serial here, and Christie made the first Westerns on the West Coast using Griffith Park for backgrounds. These films were rarely longer than two reels.

The Nestor Studio was located in the former Blondeau Tavern on the northwest corner of Sunset Boulevard and Gower Street. In 1912, the Nestor Company became part of Universal Pictures. Three years later, the lot at the site of the former Blondeau Tavern became the Christie Hollywood Studio, where comedy films were made for various distributors.

Across the street from Nestor was the original site of Universal Pictures, established in 1912. After Universal moved its production units to the San Fernando Valley in 1915, it installed the L-KO Comedy unit at its former lot. By 1916, the Stern Brothers Century Comedy unit was also housed at this studio. The property later became the home of the Sunset-Gower Field baseball stadium after the studio was gutted by fire in 1926.

In 1913, the Kennedy Feature Film Company took over an existing studio building and stage on Gordon Street, just south of Sunset Boulevard, and made a five-reel feature film entitled *Charlotte Corday*. The property was later leased to other independents, such as Fred Balshofer of the Yorke Film Company and the Bulls Eye Film Corporation.

That same year, the Jesse Lasky Feature Play Company came to Hollywood and leased an old barn, laboratory, and stage on the southeast corner of Selma Avenue and Vine Street. It was here the company made its first film, *The Squaw Man*, directed by Oscar Apfel and Cecil B. DeMille. A box office blockbuster, it was the first five-reel "feature" Western made in the Hollywood area.

NESTOR STUDIOS, 1913. While many studios had begun operations previously around Southern California, the Nestor Studios, located on the northwest corner of Sunset Boulevard and Gower Street, has the distinction of being the very first studio in Hollywood. David and William Horsley sent Al Christie west from the headquarters of their Centaur Film Company in New Jersey to oversee the new studio. Christie managed the three divisions of Nestor—Westerns, comedies,

and dramas—which each produced a new film every week. Nestor was taken over by Universal in 1912. Al Christie worked for a time at Universal after the merger before returning to the former Blondeau Tavern to independently produce his Christie Comedies. The studio site stayed in operation under a variety of owners until 1935, when it was razed to make room for Columbia Square, the West Coast headquarters of CBS Radio.

FORMER NESTOR STUDIOS, 1915 AND 1916. The sign out front of the former Nestor Studios changed often throughout the 1910s. Two of the tenants that moved in during that decade were the Quality Pictures Corporation in 1915 (above) and the Christie Comedies Studio the following year. Quality was headed up by former Bison Film Company manager Fred Balshofer. After leaving Bison, Balshofer worked for a time at the Sterling Motion Picture Company, the new studio home of former Keystone star Ford Sterling, before it went under in 1915. He then moved up the street to Quality. Balshofer had a long career in Hollywood before passing away in 1969 at the age of 91. Beginning in 1916, the Christie Comedies Studio (below) occupied the former Nestor/Quality studio.

CHRISTIE STUDIOS, 1927. The former Nestor lot changed greatly during the tenure of Christie Studios, as seen in this photograph from 1927. Al Christie began working in Hollywood with the Nestor Studios. For a time, he worked at Carl Laemmle's Universal Studios after Nestor was acquired by Universal in 1912. Al and his brother Charles later went independent, producing their Christie Comedies from the former Nestor lot. Their product was in such demand that the Christie brothers were able to expand and modernize their studio. They became very wealthy until losing their fortunes, including their studio, during the Great Depression.

AMALGAMATED STUDIOS, 1936. A rental lot named Amalgamated Studios, pictured here in 1936, occupied the former Nestor/ Quality/Christie Studio lot before being demolished to make way for the new CBS Columbia Square, which opened in 1938. Columbia Square was the West Coast headquarters of CBS Radio for decades, home to such radio luminaries as Jack Benny, Burns and Allen, Red Skelton, Edgar Bergen, Jack Oakie, and Steve Allen. CBS vacated the site in 2007.

CBS COLUMBIA SQUARE, 1939. This photograph, which looks to the north, was taken a year after CBS Columbia Square opened on the north side of Sunset Boulevard near Gower Street. The $2-million complex occupied the site of Nestor Studios, Hollywood's first, which was built in 1911. In the bottom left corner is the baseball field that replaced the former Century/L-KO lot after the property burned in 1926.

UNIVERSAL FILM MANUFACTURING COMPANY, 1913. Across the street from the Nestor Studios was the first home of the newly organized Universal Film Manufacturing Company. Located on the southwest corner of Sunset Boulevard and Gower Street, this lot was used by Universal for making Westerns (notice the stagecoach in the photograph above). Universal soon moved from this lot to the Universal Oak Crest Ranch in the San Fernando Valley, the site of today's Forest Lawn Hollywood Hills Cemetery and Mount Sinai Memorial Park Cemetery. After Universal left, Henry Lehrman, who directed Charlie Chaplin's first films while with Keystone, moved his L-KO (Lehrman-Knock Out) Productions to the lot. He shared this lot with the Stern Brothers Century Film Company, and both studios released their films through Universal. The studio was gutted by fire in 1926 and later became the home of the Sunset-Gower Field baseball stadium. Today, the space is occupied by a Denny's restaurant and the Gower Gulch mini-mall.

CENTURY/L-KO STUDIOS, 1921. Henry Lehrman began his movie career at Biograph in New York. He later joined Mack Sennett at Keystone in Edendale, where he acted and directed. Lehrman and original Keystone Cop Ford Sterling soon left Keystone. The two men formed their own company, but the partnership quickly dissolved. This was a common occurrence for Lehrman, who was known for his stinginess, combative nature, and for being incapable of getting along with anybody for very long. He next created the L-KO (Lehrman-Knock Out) Company, pictured in 1921; however, he did not last long here either. By 1917, he was working for William Fox producing Sunshine Comedies. Lehrman earned a reputation for putting his actors in harm's way, threatening life and limb for laughs. Comic Billie Ritchie died from injuries sustained by an attacking ostrich while filming a Lehrman comedy. Lehrman died from a heart attack in 1946 and was buried next to his former girlfriend, starlet Virginia Rappe, a woman who died at a party hosted by Roscoe "Fatty" Arbuckle in 1921. The ensuing scandal ended Arbuckle's career and helped bring censorship to the movies. This photograph shows the former Universal Studios lot on the southwest corner of Gower Street and Sunset Boulevard, which became the Century/L-KO lot in 1916.

L-KO Studio, 1916. This photograph, taken on April 22, 1916, shows the cast and crew members of the Lehrman-Knock Out (L-KO) Company. Frank "Fatty" Voss, the studio's star, is seen in the back row in the center, between the two middle cameras. The rotund Voss was L-KO's answer to Keystone's Roscoe "Fatty" Arbuckle. Voss died of heart failure at the age of 30, exactly one year after this photograph was taken.

Century/L-KO Studio, 1920. This aerial shot, looking southeast, shows the studio shared by the Century Film and L-KO companies. Tree-lined Sunset Boulevard is on the left, with Gower Street paralleling the top of the photograph. L-KO operated out of the west side of the studio (closest to the bottom), while Century was on the opposite side of the lot bordering Gower Street. Nestor Studios, Hollywood's first, is barely visible on the far left of the photograph.

NESTOR RANCH, 1911. After Universal vacated its Hollywood lot on the southwest corner of Sunset Boulevard and Gower Street, it moved for a time to a parcel of land near Burbank overlooking the San Fernando Valley. It was known as Nestor Ranch, which had previously been used by Nestor Studios. It was renamed Universal Oak Crest Ranch after Nestor's properties were incorporated into the new conglomerate. It was here that the battle scenes for D.W. Griffith's still-controversial epic *The Birth of a Nation* (1915) were filmed. Universal relinquished control of the ranch after its new studio, located two miles to the west in Universal City, opened in 1915. The following year, it became Lasky Ranch, a popular filming site for Paramount films. Today, it is the Forest Lawn Hollywood Hills Cemetery and Mount Sinai Memorial Park Cemetery. Pictured here, the studio heads, crewmembers, and actors from Nestor Studios are gathered for a group shot at Nestor Ranch in 1911. In the front row, second from the left, stands Nestor director-general Al Christie. Nestor president David Horlsey is fourth from the right, with his son Stanley Nestor Horsley, the namesake of the studio, at his side.

UNIVERSAL CITY, 1915 AND 1916. In 1913, Universal Studios founder Carl Laemmle opened his Universal City on the Universal Oak Crest Ranch. Laemmle also added a zoo to the property to provide animals for his films and to generate revenue as a tourist attraction. The new studio soon proved inadequate, so Laemmle shelled out $165,000 for the 230-acre Taylor Ranch, located two miles to the west, where he rebuilt his studio/city. It opened to great fanfare on March 15, 1915. Below is a photograph of the new Universal City after a rare snowfall in 1916.

KENNEDY FEATURES FILM CORP., 1914. Just two blocks away from the old Nestor Studios was the Kennedy Features lot at 1339 Gordon Street (pictured above), located just south of Sunset Boulevard. The "Features" portion of the studio's name was not false advertising. It was here in 1914 that *Charlotte Corday*, one of the earliest five-reel feature-length films ever shot in Hollywood, was made. The photograph below shows filming of *Charlotte Corday*, which was a French Revolution story. In later years, the Kennedy lot would also be home to Loftus Studios and Gordon Street Studios before being integrated, like most of the surrounding area, into Columbia Pictures.

YORKE FILM CORP., 1915 AND 1917. Next door to Kennedy was the Yorke Film Corporation (above), located at the northwest corner of Gordon Street and Fountain Avenue at 1329 Gordon Street. Fred Balshofer formed Yorke after he left Edendale's Bison Studios, where he was the company manager. For a time, Balshofer also ran the Sterling Motion Picture Company from this site. This was the short-lived home of former Keystone comic Ford Sterling, one of the original Keystone Cops, who was supplanted as the biggest star on Mack Sennett's roster the day Charlie Chaplin arrived in Edendale. Balshofer later formed Balshofer Studios on the site with his own bevy of bathing beauties (below).

BULLS EYE FILM CORP., 1919. Another renter of the lot at 1329 Gordon Street was the Bulls Eye Film Corporation (above). The Bulls Eye Comedies starred Billy West (below), who was the world's leading Charlie Chaplin impersonator. West, who was born in Russia as Roy B. Weissberg, was so good at imitating the Little Tramp that he was never sued by Chaplin, a clear sign of respect, as it was common for Charlie to litigate the less accomplished impersonators. West performed in Hollywood for many years. During the latter part of his life, he worked steps away from his old haunts at Bulls Eye, as he was employed on the Columbia Pictures lot as an assistant director and the manager of the Columbia Grill.

THE JESSE L. LASKY FEATURE PLAY COMPANY, 1913. On December 29, 1913, the members of the Lasky company began their initial day of filming for *The Squaw Man*, the first full-length Western feature ever shot in Hollywood. Cecil B. DeMille (seen in the middle of the photograph, wearing a hat and riding boots with his hand in his belt) had this photograph taken, knowing full well the historical significance of what was about to take place.

THE JESSE L. LASKY FEATURE PLAY COMPANY, 1915. The building DeMille used to stage *The Squaw Man*—known today as the Lasky-DeMille Barn, which serves as the headquarters of the preservation organization known as Hollywood Heritage—was located on the southeast corner of Vine Street and Selma Avenue, pictured here in 1915. DeMille sublet the property for $250 a month from Harry Revier and L.L. Burns.

THE JESSE L. LASKY FEATURE PLAY COMPANY, 1914. The box office receipts from *The Squaw Man* ($245,000 against only $15,000 in costs) funded other Lasky features in 1914, including *The Virginian*. The barn/stage was in a citrus grove at the time, and the property is still heavily wooded in the photograph above. The below photograph, from *The Call Of The North*, captures Cecil B. DeMille (standing, second from right) directing mid-pantomime. The success of the early Lasky features put the studio on a much firmer footing than most of its Poverty Row neighbors. Within two years, Lasky would merge with Adolph Zukor's Famous Players Film Company to create what would eventually be known to the world as Paramount Pictures.

Three

GOWER GULCH AND THE BEACHWOOD DRIVE STUDIOS

There is no gulch at the corner of Sunset Boulevard and Gower Street. This area only took on the nickname "Gower Gulch" after 1939's fatal "dry-gulching" (shooting in the back) of stuntman Johnny Tyke by fellow movie cowboy Jack Ward.

It was at this intersection that film cowboys frequented the Columbia Drugs and Fountain, where agents secured jobs for the cinema cowpokes from the various independent studios in and around Sunset Boulevard and Gower Street.

In 1919, William Horsley, who opened the Nestor Studios with his brother David in 1911, built a studio/laboratory/office building near the southeast corner of Gower Street and Sunset Boulevard. Horsley leased the property to independent companies into the 1940s, when Jerry Fairbanks Productions took it over to make shorts for Paramount.

Universal star Francis Ford, the brother of director John Ford, built his own studio in 1919 on the southeast corner of Sunset Boulevard and today's Beachwood Drive. In 1926, the Stern Film Company moved into the former Francis Ford Studio after its lot burned down and continued to make its Stern Bros. Comedies here into the 1930s.

Prior to 1921, Beachwood Drive was known as Acacia Street, an unpaved alley between Gower Street (to the west) and Gordon Street (to the east). One of the first to build a studio on the street was Russell Productions. Following Russell at 1439 Beachwood Drive were Harry Joe Brown, Crown, Norman Dawn, Goodman, Goodwill, Granada, Hutchinson, Morante, and Ben Wilson Productions. This rental facility later became a part of the Columbia studio lot.

In 1922, the Kinemart Production Company occupied the premises at 1442 Beachwood Drive, across the street from the Russell Studio. Later, this studio would host Sanford Productions, Hercules, Historical Productions, and Barsky Productions.

Other independents on Beachwood Drive at this time included O.K. Productions and Rayart Pictures, a forerunner of Monogram. The studio just south of Kinemart at 1424–1426 Beachwood Drive housed Phil Goldstone Productions in 1922. Sam Bischoff acquired this studio for Bischoff Comedies in 1924. Later, the Cohn brothers of Columbia Pictures purchased the property.

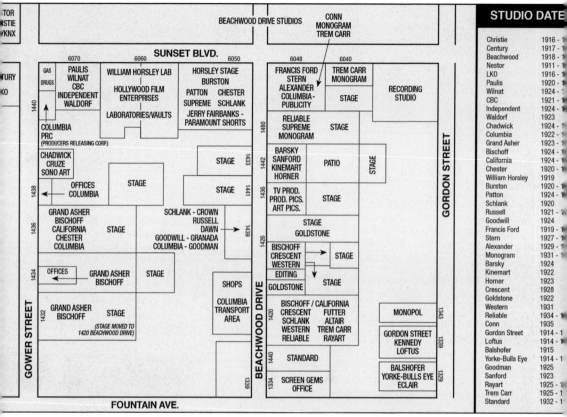

GOWER GULCH MAP, 1920S AND 1930S. After Nestor Studios (upper left corner of the map) opened in 1911, studios began popping up nearby, primarily on the south side of Sunset Boulevard east of Gower Street. During these frenetic early years of Hollywood's Poverty Row, sign painters were kept busy changing the names on the buildings as producers and studios swapped addresses in a frenzied, shell game–esque series of moves. In at least one case, an entire building changed address as well. This was the property at 1432 North Gower Street (lower left of the map) that is listed here as belonging to both Grand-Asher and Bischoff. When Samuel Bischoff purchased the property in 1924, he was shocked to learn that he had not bought the ground beneath it, which was controlled by Columbia chief Harry Cohn. The entire stage was picked up and moved one block to the east to 1420 Beachwood Drive. This building eventually became Columbia's Stage 7, home to *The Three Stooges* and *The Monkees*.

HOLLYWOOD, 1920. This aerial shot looking east shows Vine Street running left to right at the bottom, with Sunset Boulevard cutting across diagonally. At the lower portion of the photograph is the Famous Players–Lasky (FPL) Studios, which would soon be known to the world as Paramount Pictures. At the center of the photograph, just above the FPL backlots, is the Christie Studio, the site of Hollywood's first studio. Across Sunset Boulevard to the right is the L-KO and Century lot. This was the site of Universal's first home before they moved to Universal Oak Crest Ranch in 1913. Just above this site, across Gower Street, are the studios that would soon come together under the Columbia Pictures banner. The open lot at the top of the photograph would soon be the first permanent home of Warner Bros. It is where *The Jazz Singer*, the first successful commercial talkie film, was produced in 1927. Amazingly, the site of Hollywood's first studio, the spot where the sound era began, and the birthplaces of Hollywood powerhouses Paramount, Universal, Warner Bros., and Columbia, can all be seen in the same photograph.

GOWER STREET AND SUNSET BOULEVARD (LOOKING SOUTH), 1932. Much changed in the intervening two decades since this intersection was the site of the first Hollywood studio. In a remarkably short time, it transformed from a semirural crossing into a busy city intersection. It was here, just to the right, that Nestor Studios (not visible in the photograph) was founded in 1911. The corner on the upper right was shared by the Stern Brothers Century Comedy unit and Henry Lehrman's L-KO (Lehrman-Knock Out) Comedies for many years before becoming a stadium used by baseball teams from the different studios. The corner on the upper left-hand side of the photograph shows Columbia Drugs and Fountain, an eatery frequented by cowboys scrounging for Western jobs in one of the local studios. Behind it is Columbia Pictures. This intersection came to be known as "Gower Gulch" after Johnny Tyke was "dry-gulched" (shot in the back) here in 1938 by fellow cowboy stuntman Jack Ward.

GOWER STREET AND SUNSET BOULEVARD, 1923 AND 1920. Pictured above is the same intersection looking towards the northwest from south of Sunset Boulevard. In the upper portion is a view of the Christie Studios, formerly Nestor Studios. The bottom left is the site of the Century/L-KO unit, with the Gower Street lots that would eventually all be incorporated into Columbia Pictures in the foreground. Below is a shot of the backlots at the Century/L-KO lot two years earlier. Universal executives Abe and Julius Stern created the Lehrman-Knock Out company in 1916. The following year, they formed the Century Comedy Company and installed them both on the same lot. Below, comedian Monty Banks (facing the camera at far right) inspects filming at L-KO in 1920.

45

Wm. Horsley Studios, 1921 and 1925. Brothers David Horsley and William Horsley formed the first studio in Hollywood in 1911. A few years later, William established a film processing lab and studio here at 6050 and 6060 Sunset Boulevard, as seen in the above architectural drawing from 1921. The studio became the home to several independent production houses throughout the 1920s, including Patton, Chester, Supreme, Schlank, Burston, CBC (Columbia), and others. The lab later became home to the Hollywood Film Enterprises Laboratory for many years. Today, the building houses a videography facility.

SCHLANK STUDIO, 1920. Morris R. Schlank Productions started out on Poverty Row in 1920 by leasing stage and office space in the Horsley Studio at 6050 Sunset Boulevard. Over the next few years, Schlank made Hank Mann comedies both here and at the Russell Studio at 1439 Beachwood Drive and at the Bischoff Studio at 1420 Beachwood Drive. In the photograph above, Hank Mann (left) sits next to Morris R. Schlank (right), while three unidentified gentlemen look on. Mann had 430 film credits in a career that lasted until 1960. He is best remembered today as Charlie Chaplin's boxing opponent in *City Lights* (1931). In the photograph below, Mann (center) is seen during filming of *The Blacksmith* (1920), which was shot at one of the Beachwood Drive studios.

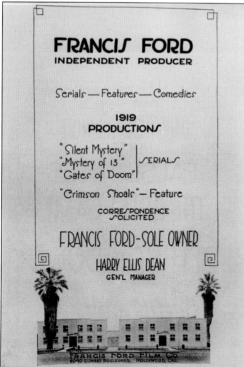

JERRY FAIRBANKS/PARAMOUNT SHORT SUBJECTS, 1945. The former Horsley Studios at 6050 Sunset Boulevard was home to many film companies, including the Jerry Fairbanks/Paramount Short Subjects (above). As head of Paramount's shorts division, Fairbanks produced shows like *Television Films*, *Popular Science*, *Speaking of Animals*, *Unusual Occupations*, and *Institutional Films*.

FRANCIS FORD ADVERTISEMENT, 1919. This ad from 1919 shows a drawing of Francis Ford's studio with a listing of the three serials—*Silent Mystery*, *Mystery of 13*, and *Gates of Doom*—and one feature, *Crimson Shoals*, currently being filmed at the studio. Ford not only supplied the stages but also directed and starred in most of these productions as well.

FRANCIS FORD STUDIO, 1920.
Universal actor-director Francis
Ford (the older brother of
director John Ford) and his
partner Louis Burston built the
studio above on the southeast
corner of Sunset Boulevard
and Beachwood Drive in 1919.
Burston, pictured at right in
an advertisement from 1920,
was killed in an automobile
crash in 1921. Afterwards, Ford
continued to operate out of half
of the complex at 6048 Sunset
Boulevard, with the other half
leased out to independent
productions. Ford would later
leave this building behind,
relocating at Universal Studios
in the San Fernando Valley.

STUDIO

BURSTON FILMS INC.
HOLLYWOOD, CAL.

BIGGER and BETTER pictures for the
the coming year.

My personal supervision will be given to all
productions.

EXHIBITORS and EXCHANGEMEN
are assured of pictures of artistic excellence
and box office value.

LOUIS BURSTON, President
BURSTON FILMS Inc.

Longacre Building   6050 Sunset Boulevard
New York City   Los Angeles, Cal.

FRANCIS FORD STUDIO, 1922. Francis Ford and Ella Hall are being entertained by a seal on the front lawn of the Francis Ford Studio at 6040 Sunset Boulevard. Ford was not only a producer but an actor as well, with over 400 film credits. He often appeared in his younger brother John's films, including such classics as *Young Mr. Lincoln* (1939) and *The Quiet Man* (1952). He died in 1953 at the age of 72.

SUNSET BOULEVARD STUDIOS, 1920. This rare 1920 aerial photograph looks southeast and shows the early studios fronting Sunset Boulevard. On the left is Sunset Boulevard, with Gower Street at the bottom, Gordon Street at the top, and a barely visible Beachwood Drive in the middle. The white buildings fronting Sunset Boulevard are, from top to bottom, Francis Ford Studios, Horsley Studios, and the Horsley Laboratory. The former Nestor Studios is across Sunset Boulevard on the left, with Century/L-KO at the bottom right.

STERN FILM COMPANY STUDIO, 1927 AND 1928. Universal unit managers Julius and Abe Stern moved their Century Comedy Company from the southwest corner of Gower Street and Sunset Boulevard to the Francis Ford Studio in 1926 after a fire razed the Century/L-KO Studio. Above, a group of studio personnel poses out front. Below, producer Max Alexander poses with Doreen Turner (left) and Arthur Trimble, the stars of the Buster Brown series of juvenile comedies that the Stern Film Company produced for Universal.

RELIABLE PICTURES, 1935. During the mid-1930s, Reliable Pictures was housed in the former Stern Film/Francis Ford Studio at 6048 Sunset Boulevard. Reliable specialized in B-Westerns starring Richard Talmadge, Tom Tyler, Rin Tin Tin Jr., and Jack Perrin. Some of their films include *The Cactus Kid, The Live Wire, Born to Battle, Fast Bullets, Pinto Rustlers, The Silver Trail,* and *Santa Fe Rides.* Reliable Pictures was the cocreation of Hollywood veterans Harry S. Webb and Bernard B. Ray.

BEACHWOOD DRIVE, 1950. This view looking north up Beachwood Drive shows Columbia Stage 7 (lower right), which was originally located a block to the west at the California Studios of Samuel Bischoff before it was moved here. At the far end of the block is the Stern Film Company (later Reliable Pictures Corporation), which was located at 1480 Beachwood Drive and Sunset Boulevard.

SUNSET AND GOWER, 1939. This view looking southeast at the intersection of Sunset Boulevard and Gower Street shows the heart of Poverty Row. On the southeast corner of the intersection is Columbia Drug and Fountain, where many actors, directors, and other workers regularly congregated to look for day work at the nearby studios. Adjacent to the drugstore is the former Independent Studio next to Horsley Laboratories (Hollywood Film Enterprises). Next door, at Beachwood Drive, is the Horsley Studio, which was then home to Jerry Fairbanks/Paramount Shorts Studios.

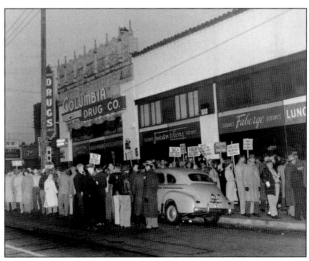

SUNSET AND GOWER, 1946. This view of Columbia Drug and Fountain on the southeast corner of Sunset Boulevard and Gower Street shows studio workers striking against Columbia Pictures, whose administrative offices were just steps to the south. By this time, the intersection had taken on the nickname "Gower Gulch" after a shooting in the back ("dry-gulching") of a studio cowboy occurred here.

Sunset and Gower, 1936. Gower Gulch cowboys gather on the corner of Sunset Boulevard and Gower Street hoping to be cast in a B-Western filming nearby. Many of the studios in the area specialized in Westerns. This was especially true of the Reliable Pictures Corporation, which was housed in the former Stern Film/Francis Ford Studio at 6048 Sunset Boulevard.

Independent Studios, 1923. Located at 6070 Sunset Boulevard, this studio was managed by producer Jesse J. Goldburg. At the time of this photograph, one of the tenants here was CBC (Cohn-Brandt-Cohn), the forerunner of Columbia Pictures. In fact, 6070 Sunset Boulevard is considered by some historians to be the actual birthplace of Columbia.

PRC Studios, 1942. Producers Releasing Corporation (PRC), at 1140 North Gower Street, made nearly 200 films during the eight years (1939–1947) that it existed and reportedly never spent more than $100,000 on any of them. The output of studio heads Sigmund Neufeld and Sam Newfield (actual brothers with differently spelled surnames) was often of such low quality that many claimed PRC actually stood for "Poverty Row Crap." While the majority of PRC's output could be described as substandard, the studio did employ an impressive array of stars, including Lash LaRue, Buster Crabbe, Bela Lugosi, Lionel Atwill, Bob Steele, Fuzzy St. John, and Bob Livingston. The studio occasionally produced the rare gem, like 1945's noir thriller *Detour*, which was selected in 1992 by the National Registry for preservation for being either "culturally, historically or aesthetically significant."

BARSKY STUDIO, 1926. Bud Barsky was already a well-known Hollywood producer when he formed Bud Barsky Productions in 1924. Barsky housed his independent productions at three Poverty Row studios: California/Bischoff at 1434 North Gower Street, Grand-Asher at 1436 North Gower Street, and at the Kinemart Studio at 1442 Beachwood Drive. Above, Barsky (center, wearing a striped tie) stands among the cast and crew of *The Law of the Snow Country* (1926), which starred Noble Johnson and Kenneth MacDonald. To the left is a poster for Barsky's 1926 production *Roaring Road*, which starred Kenneth MacDonald and Jane Thomas and was directed by Paul Hurst.

WESTERN PICTURES CORPORATION, 1935. Beachwood Drive was once a dirt alley named Acacia Street. In 1921, it was paved and renamed. Three years later, this building at 1420 North Beachwood Drive became the property of producer Samuel Bischoff, who called it California Studio. Over the next several years, a seemingly endless stream of producers worked out of the complex, including Altair Productions, Beacon, De Villard, B.A. Goodman, Al Nathan, Progress, Sovereign Features, Trem Carr, Granada, Gold Medal, Al Herman, Pathfinder, Romance, Ben Wilson Productions, Kinemart, Trinity Pictures, Yaconelli, Color Craft, American Eagle, Big Chief, Unique Screen Arts, Cardinal, United Color, Pacific Pictures, Fowler, Charles J. Davis, Standard, Freeman-Lang, Bennet-King, Goldsmith Productions, and the General Pictures Corporation. Western Pictures Corporation, seen here, occupied this building in 1935. A year later, Columbia Pictures began making shorts here and eventually purchased the building, renaming it Stage 7, where the Columbia shorts were filmed, including many by the Three Stooges. By 1941, Columbia had acquired all the surrounding buildings on both sides of the street and converted Beachwood Drive into a private road inside its new studio complex.

CALIFORNIA STUDIO–SAM BISCHOFF, 1926. The Grand-Asher Company purchased the California Studio at 1436 North Gower Street (above) from C.A. Chester in 1923. Grand-Asher later built another stage south of the California Studio at 1432 North Gower Street. In 1924, Samuel Bischoff purchased the south stage owned by Grand-Asher (below). Two years later, Bischoff relocated this building a block to the east at 1420 North Beachwood Drive. This move was prompted when Bischoff learned that he had purchased the building at 1432 North Gower but not the ground beneath it. These rights were held by Columbia chief Harry Cohn, which led to a protracted legal fight before Bischoff threw in the towel and moved the entire building.

JAMES CRUZE STUDIO, 1930. Director James Cruze located his production company in the former Chadwick Studio building at 1440 Gower Street in 1928. The studio was outfitted with sound equipment. Cruze produced several independent films here, including *The Night Flyer*, *The Red Mark*, *Hello Sister*, *The Big Fight*, *The Costello Case*, *Command Performance*, *Hell Bound*, and *The Great Gabbo*.

COLUMBIA STUDIO PUBLICITY DEPARTMENT, 1938. This building at 1442 North Gower Street was once the headquarters for PRC (Producers Releasing Corporation), which produced hundreds of films in the Gower Street and Beachwood Drive studios over the years (see page 55). It later became Columbia's publicity department after Columbia initiated the purchase of most of the buildings in the area.

STAGE 7, 1935. Columbia's new Stage 7 was the same building that Samuel Bischoff was forced to move from Gower Street in a land dispute with Harry Cohn. After it was acquired by Columbia, it was quickly put into service as the home of Columbia shorts. The photograph above shows a scene from the Three Stooges, who worked out of Stage 7 for many years. In this scene, Moe Howard grabs a watermelon from the back of a truck with Larry Fine (with his back turned) on the sidewalk to the right. Stage 7 can be seen farther down the block, across the street on the left. Below, the Columbia production of *Mr. Smith Goes To Washington* (1939) uses the studio's backlot adjacent to Stage 7 to model the fictional town of Jackson City during a political parade.

STAGE 7, 1934 AND 1947. Long before purchasing the property in 1941, Columbia leased Stage 7 (right) to serve as the home of its shorts division. In the staged photograph below, a wardrobe man rushes a new outfit to actor Ron Randell, publicizing the fact that Randell, in a remarkable feat of multitasking, was working on four films simultaneously! These films were *It Had To Be You* with Ginger Rogers, *Bulldog Drummond Strikes Back*, *The Mating of Millie*, and *The Sign of the Ram*. Randell is pictured next to the Stage 7 doorway at 1420 Beachwood Drive. In the 1960s, Stage 7 was used by Columbia's Screen Gems Television division and was home to shows like *The Monkees*.

GRAND-ASHER STUDIOS, 1923 AND 1926. Grand-Asher Productions purchased the office building at 1434 North Gower Street (above, far left) and stage at 1432 North Gower Street (right) from the Chester Comedy Company around 1923 (seen here in the photograph above). Between 1924 and 1926, the office and stage were home to Bischoff Productions, H.C. Witwer Comedies, "Biff" Thrill Comedies, and Gold Medal Comedies. Below, Grand-Asher personnel pose together. Seated from left to right are producer Joe Rock, producer Sam Grand, and star Monty Banks. Production manager Jack Mintz stands behind them.

IT HAPPENED IN HOLLYWOOD, 1937. A studio security guard surveys filming for 1937's *It Happened In Hollywood*, which was shot on Beachwood Drive looking north (the Hollywood sign is barely visible in the distance). *It Happened In Hollywood* was a tale of the turbulent transition from silents to talkies that Hollywood experienced a decade earlier. In the film, silent cowboy star Tim Bart, played by Richard Dix, loses his big-time career when the new recording processes force his studio to move its filming indoors, thereby killing off Westerns. Fay Wray plays Gloria Gay, Bart's leading lady, whose career reaches new heights in the sound era. Below, a prop billboard advertises Gay's film *The Devil's Doorway*. This spot, at 1339 Beachwood Drive, was located on the west side of the street, just north of Fountain Avenue.

WILNAT STUDIO, 1924. Located at 1329 Gordon Street, Wilnat Films was making a Hallroom Boys Comedy at the time of these photographs. Above, four gentlemen pose in the Wilnat's doorway, including CBC heads Harry Cohn (white shirt) and Jack Cohn (white pants). Shortly afterwards, Wilnat moved to the Paulis-Independent Studio at 6070 Sunset Boulevard to produce Billy West Comedies. CBC, the forerunner of Columbia Pictures, was named after the initials of its founders, Harry Cohn, Joe Brandt, and Jack Cohn. Known for its stinginess, CBC was commonly referred to as "corned beef and cabbage," a low-budget Depression-era meal. Below, CBC vice-president Harry Cohn (left) is seen standing in the doorway with Billy West, with three unidentified women in the foreground.

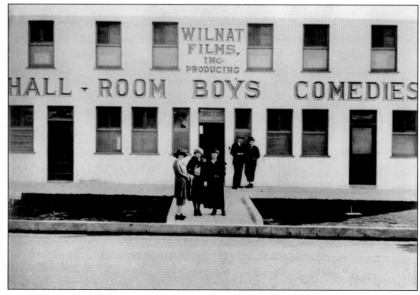

RKO, 1928. While considered more of a mini-major than a typical Poverty Row studio, RKO Radio Pictures inhabited a studio on Gower Street for decades. The 13-acre RKO lot opened in 1919 as the Robertson-Cole Studios. In 1922, the studio changed its name to the Film Booking Office (FBO). Banker Joseph P. Kennedy, the father of future US president John F. Kennedy, bought the studio for $1 million in 1926 and later sold it to the Radio Corporation of America (RCA) in 1928. FBO later merged with the Keith-Albee-Orpheum (KAO) vaudeville circuit, forming Radio-Keith-Orpheum (RKO) Pictures. RKO became the most modest of the major studios of the era, home to Fred Astaire, Ginger Rogers, *King Kong*, and *Citizen Kane*. RKO was later driven into the ground by its increasingly erratic owner, Howard Hughes. He sold it to the General Tire and Rubber Company in 1955, which in turn sold it to Desi Arnaz and Lucille Ball's Desilu Productions two years later. In 1967, Ball sold the studio to Paramount Pictures, which shared the same city block with RKO.

DESILU, 1959. Pictured here is a shot of the Desilu Studios (the former RKO lot) looking north along Gower Street (left), with Melrose Avenue at the bottom. Lucille Ball and Desi Arnaz owned this property for 10 years. For decades, Paramount had shared the same city block with the 13-acre former RKO Radio Pictures Studio. After Lucille Ball sold the property to Paramount in 1967, the two lots were ceremonially joined during a special ribbon-cutting ceremony where Ball cut film stock with oversized scissors.

GOWER GULCH SHOPPING CENTER, 1992. After the Century/L-KO Studio burned to the ground in 1926, the property was used as a baseball field. By the 1970s, the property was developed into the Gower Gulch shopping center, "Home of the Stars." In 1992, the Gower Gulch "Walk of Fame" was inaugurated here in the sidewalk fronting the stores, honoring some of the famous actors who worked nearby in Poverty Row studios.

Four

EAST HOLLYWOOD'S POVERTY ROW

The Kinemacolor Film Company opened its studio in 1911 on a former farm on the southwest corner of what is now Virgil Avenue and Sunset Boulevard in East Hollywood. Two years later, the studio was taken over by the Reliance Film Company, later known as Majestic-Reliance and still later as the Triangle–Fine Arts Company of D.W. Griffith. It was here that Griffith made his silent epics *The Birth of a Nation* (1915) and *Intolerance* (1916).

This studio later became a rental lot for independent companies until 1927, when it became the Tiffany-Stahl Studio during the birth of talkies. In later years, this studio lot became known as the Talisman Studio, where independent producers leased office and stage space. Around 1940, Columbia purchased the Talisman lot, renaming it Sunset Studio, where productions like *The Three Stooges*, *Whistler*, *Lone Wolf*, and other Columbia features and shorts were produced. During the late 1960s, this historic studio lot was demolished to make way for a market.

William Fox began making films in Fort Lee, New Jersey, before moving west to the old Selig studio in Edendale in 1914. The following year, he moved his operations to a lot at the corner of Sunset Boulevard and Western Avenue in Hollywood.

Nearby in 1913, the Vitagraph Company of America moved from Santa Monica (where it opened a studio in 1911) to a plot of land at the northeast corner of Prospect and Talmadge Streets. After Vitagraph merged with Warner Bros. in 1925, this lot was known as the Warner Bros. East Hollywood Studio Annex. By the 1950s, it had become the ABC Television Center. Today, it is known as Prospect Studios, which is owned by the Walt Disney Company.

Silent comedienne Mabel Normand had her own studio at the intersection of Fountain and Bates Avenues and Effie Street in 1916. This lot was later owned by William S. Hart.

A few blocks away was the Lubin/Essanay Studio, which opened in 1912 at the corner of Hoover Street and Sunset Boulevard. A succession of film companies later owned the property, including Kalem, Jean Navelle, Charles Ray, International/Like Studio, Monogram Pictures, and Allied Artists. For many years, this property was home to public television's KCET. Today, it serves as the media center for the Church of Scientology.

RELIANCE STUDIO, 1914. In 1911, the Kinemacolor Film Company opened a studio on a former farm on the southwest corner of today's Virgil Avenue and Sunset Boulevard in East Hollywood. Two years later, the studio was taken over by the Reliance Film Company, later known as Majestic-Reliance and still later as the Triangle–Fine Arts Company of D.W. Griffith, which Griffith became a part of after leaving Biograph. It was here that Griffith made his silent epics *The Birth of a Nation*

(1915) and *Intolerance* (1916). This studio later became a rental lot for independent companies until 1927, when it became the Tiffany-Stahl Studio. Later, it was known as the Talisman Studio, where independent producers leased office and stage space. Around 1940, Columbia purchased the Talisman lot, renaming it Sunset Studio. Today, a market occupies the site.

TRIANGLE–FINE ARTS STUDIO, 1916. Kentucky-native David Wark Griffith got his first job in films in 1907 as an actor at the Edison Studios in the Bronx. Moving on to Biograph, Griffith was soon handed a camera, and he began directing what would eventually be around 450 films over the course of his career. Tiring of restrictions placed on him by Biograph higher-ups, Griffith moved to the former Reliance-Majestic Studios to set up his own leg of Triangle Studios with Thomas Ince and Mack Sennett. It was here that Griffith created 1915's still-controversial epic *The Birth of a Nation*, one of the biggest blockbusters of the entire silent era. In response to criticism generated by the film's overt racism, Griffith filmed *Intolerance* the following year; it was a lavish epic showing the effects of intolerance during four different periods in history. The Babylonian sets built for the film were some of the most massive ever created. They are pictured above during construction on the northeast corner of Hillhurst Drive and Sunset Boulevard, which was across the street from Griffith's studio lot.

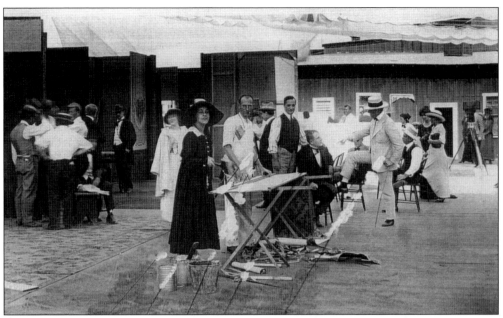

TRIANGLE–FINE ARTS STUDIO, 1916. In the photograph above, famed Russian actress Alla Nazimova (center) pays a visit to D.W. Griffith's studio in 1916. To the right, Griffith can be seen with his leg up, conversing with his production staff. Below, a crowd of cinematic cowboys fronted by Douglas Fairbanks (center, brandishing two guns), Bessie Love (to the right of Fairbanks), and director Allan Dwan (holding a megaphone) pose on one of the large Triangle–Fine Arts stages during filming of 1916's *The Good Bad Man*. Fairbanks not only starred in this film but wrote and produced it as well. Victor Fleming, who was 27 years old at the time, was the film's cinematographer. Fleming would later become a legendary director, helming both *Gone With the Wind* and *The Wizard of Oz* in the same year (1939).

VIEWS OF
TIFFANY-STAHL STUDIOS
HOLLYWOOD, CAL.

TIFFANY-STAHL STUDIOS, 1928 AND 1929. Located at the intersection of Sunset and Hollywood Boulevards and Virgil Avenue in East Hollywood, the former Reliance-Majestic and Triangle–Fine Arts Studio became Tiffany Pictures in 1927. Tiffany was founded in 1921 by movie star Mae Murray and director John M. Stahl. Stahl later took over the company and renamed the studio Tiffany-Stahl, pictured above and below. Over its 11-year history (1921–1932), Tiffany released 70 features, including 20 Westerns, many starring Bob Steele and Ken Maynard. After Tiffany ceased operations in 1932, Columbia Pictures bought the studio.

WILLIAM FOX STUDIOS, 1915. William Fox began making films in Fort Lee, New Jersey, before moving west to the old Selig studio in Edendale in 1914. The following year, he moved his operations to a lot at the corner of Sunset Boulevard and Western Avenue in Hollywood, which had previously been a studio owned by racist author and producer Rev. Thomas Dixon Jr., author of *The Clansman*, the book on which *The Birth of a Nation* (1915) was based. After Fox took over the space, it was greatly expanded to encompass two entire city blocks. This was the lot where Theda Bara and Tom Mix made their most important films. Fox eventually moved to West Los Angeles, leaving the old lot as a laboratory and studio annex. It was later razed, and two shopping centers now cover the site.

WILLIAM FOX STUDIO, 1921 AND 1926. Hollywood was not nearly as congested as today when the above photograph was taken in 1921. The view looks to the south along Western Avenue, with Sunset Boulevard intersecting at the bottom. In 1915, the William Fox Studio was established on the southwest corner of Sunset Boulevard and Western Avenue at 1418 North Western Avenue (on the right side of Western Avenue, with the studio's backlots across the street). The studio expanded, filling two entire city blocks. After Fox moved to West Los Angeles in 1930, the Western Avenue studio was used for making shorts. Later, it was used by 20th Century Fox Television before being demolished in 1971.

MABEL NORMAND STUDIO, 1916; WILLIAM S. HART STUDIO, 1917. Two of the biggest stars of the silent era made the same small studio in East Hollywood their cinematic homes during the mid-1910s. Diminutive comedienne Mabel Normand became a huge star at Mack Sennett's Keystone Studios. Sennett set her up with her own production facilities here at Fountain and Bates Avenues and Effie Street in 1916. Normand died at the age of 37 in 1930, her life cut short by scandal and drug abuse. William S. Hart, one of the biggest Western stars of the silent era, later owned this lot. Hart began his career as a stage actor in New York before coming to California to make Westerns for Thomas Ince. Remarkably, his first screen appearance took place when Hart was 49, an advanced age for an action star. This studio still exists as Mack Sennett Studios.

VITAGRAPH STUDIOS, 1911 AND 1914. Vitagraph, one of the very first motion picture companies, began in 1897 when reporter J. Stuart Blackton interviewed Thomas Edison, who talked Blackton into purchasing one of his projectors and some films. A short time later, using the equipment he purchased from Edison to go into direct competition with him, Blackton founded the American Vitagraph Company with his business partner Albert E. Smith. In 1911, Vitagraph established its first Southern California studio in Santa Monica at 1415 Second Street at Ocean Avenue (above). In 1913, it relocated to East Hollywood (below) at the corner of Prospect Avenue and Talmadge Street. This later became the Warner Bros. East Hollywood Annex after Warner Bros. purchased Vitagraph in 1925. WB sold it to ABC in 1948, and today it is Prospect Studios, the home of many long-running soap operas and game shows.

LUBIN FILM COMPANY STUDIO, 1912. Siegmund "Pop" Lubin was a Jewish optometrist who emigrated from Poland and became a pioneer of cinema at his state-of-the-art studio in Philadelphia that he called "Lubinville." Lubin later opened studios in Jacksonville, Florida, where Oliver Hardy, of Laurel and Hardy fame, made his screen debut. Heading west, Lubin built studios in Coronado, California, and in a former farm house in East Hollywood, pictured here, at the corner of Hoover Street and Sunset Boulevard. For years, Lubin was embroiled in a legal feud with Thomas Edison's monopolistic Film Trust before throwing in the towel and joining the syndicate. The Trust's dissolution by the Supreme Court in 1915, coupled with some bad luck, brought on Lubin's downfall. He declared bankruptcy in 1916 and spent the remainder of his life working again as an optometrist.

KALEM STUDIO, 1915. After Lubin's departure, the Kalem Company moved into the former Lubin studio in East Hollywood. Kalem was founded in 1907 in New York by George Kleine, Samuel Long, and Frank J. Marion, whose initials—K, L, and M—gave the company its name. Like Lubin, Kalem was also a member of Edison's Trust. Kalem was one of the first American movie companies to film on location in Europe.

CHARLES RAY PRODUCTIONS, 1922. Charles Ray Productions was located at 1425 Fleming Street (later changed to 4376 Sunset Boulevard) in the former Kalem Studio in East Hollywood. Ray's signature feature film made here was *The Courtship of Miles Standish* (1923), reportedly one of the most expensive silent films ever made. For *Courtship*, Ray had a 180-ton replica of the *Mayflower* built here. He was said to have spent over $1 million of his own money on the film.

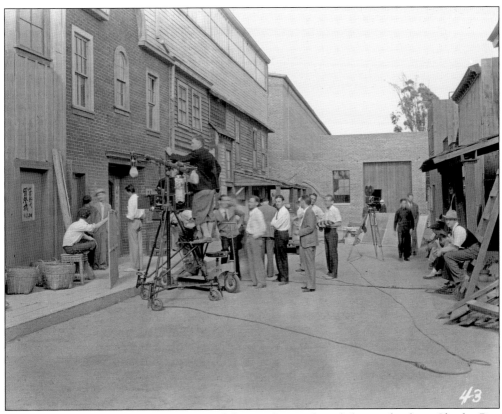

RALPH M. LIKE PRODUCTIONS, 1931. Ralph M. Like purchased this studio from Charles Ray in 1927, creating Ralph M. Like Productions. Over the next six years, Like produced a slew of Westerns, action and adventure films, and crime dramas under the Action Pictures, Mayfair Pictures, and Progressive Pictures banners. Many of these films starred his wife, Blanche Mehaffey. After leaving producing, Like returned to his old job as a studio sound engineer.

MONOGRAM STUDIO, 1936. Like so many other Hollywood enterprises, Monogram Pictures had its roots in the Poverty Row studios near Sunset Boulevard and Gower Street. Monogram cofounder Trem Carr hung his shingle here for a time at the former Francis Ford Studio at 6040–6048 Sunset Boulevard at Beachwood Drive. Monogram spent time at several other studios in the Poverty Row area before locating permanently in the former Charles Ray/Ralph M. Like studios.

MONOGRAM PICTURES, 1941. One of the best-known tenants at 4376 Sunset Boulevard was Monogram Pictures, created in the early 1930s through the merger of Trem Carr's Sono Art–World Wide Pictures and W. Ray Johnston's Rayart Productions. Monogram was famous for its low-budget action-driven Westerns. Many of them were filmed in two ranches in Placerita Canyon near Newhall, California. One is known today as the Golden Oak Ranch, which is owned by the Walt Disney Company. The other is Melody Ranch, once owned by singing cowboy Gene Autry. Melody was the home of *Gunsmoke* for the show's first six seasons until the property was destroyed by a raging brush fire. In recent years, this studio was used for the HBO series *Deadwood* and the Quentin Tarantino film *Django Unchained* (2012). Each April, this working studio is open to the public for one weekend during Santa Clarita's Cowboy Festival.

ALLIED ARTISTS STUDIOS, 1954 AND 1958. Although Monogram changed its name to Allied Artists in 1953, it still operated out of the old Monogram lot at 4376 Sunset Boulevard. Above is the administrative office, with the new name and logo on the soundstage to the left. Below, the Western backlot inside Allied is being used for *King of the Wild Stallions* (1959), which starred George Montgomery, Diane Brewster, and Edgar Buchanan. Allied Artists began as a division of Monogram in 1946, when Walter Mirisch convinced Monogram head Steve Broidy that low-budget films were on their way out and that the only way to compete with the major studios was with a division producing costlier films. In 1952, Monogram announced that going forward it would only produce films under the Allied Artists name. The following year, the Monogram name was retired.

COLORVISION STUDIOS, 1961. These studios at 4376 Sunset Boulevard in the Los Angeles district of Los Feliz first opened in 1912 as the Lubin Manufacturing Company. As one of Hollywood's longest continually operated studios, it has been owned at times by Essanay, Kalem, Jesse Hampton, Charles Ray Productions, Monogram, Allied Artists, and ColorVision. An impressive array of films and television shows have been produced here over the years, including *The Cisco Kid*, *Cosmos*, *California's Gold*, *Invasion of the Body Snatchers* (1956), *Friendly Persuasion* (1956), *House on Haunted Hill* (1959), and *El Cid* (1961). It has also been home to several hit film series, like Charlie Chan, the East Side Kids, the Bowery Boys, and the Range Busters. From 1971 to 2011, this studio was the home of public television station KCET-TV before being purchased by the Church of Scientology.

Five

MORE EARLY
HOLLYWOOD STUDIOS

In 1914, on the southeast corner of Melrose Avenue at what is now Bronson Avenue, the Fiction Players Film Company of New York purchased a farm and constructed an office, a stage, and dressing rooms. Fiction produced films on this site before being purchased by New York's Famous Players Film Corporation. Famous Players later sold the studio to former theater owner William H. Clune, who later leased the studio to other independent companies. The property still exists today and is now the home of Raleigh Studios.

In 1916, the Jesse L. Lasky Feature Play Company merged with Adolph Zukor's Famous Players Film Corporation and its distribution wing, creating what would soon be known as Paramount Pictures. A decade later, it moved from its lot at the corner of Selma Avenue and Vine Street to a larger property (formerly the Brunton/United Studio) at Melrose and Van Ness Avenues, which is still Paramount's home today.

In 1925, Al Christie of the Christie Film Company purchased Hollywood Studios and renamed it the Hollywood-Metropolitan Studios. It was here that producers like Howard Hughes and others leased space. The studio was taken over by United Artists in the late 1930s and was for a time called the General Service Studios. Today, it is known as Hollywood Center Studios.

Metro established a studio in 1915 at Lillian Way and Eleanor Street. By 1924, Metro had become part of Metro-Goldwyn-Mayer (MGM), and many of the studio buildings were moved to the new MGM lot in Culver City. The original lot where Metro started later became the studio home of classic silent comedians Charlie Chaplin and Buster Keaton.

The small Pickford-Fairbanks Studio on Santa Monica Boulevard in West Hollywood became the United Artists Studio and later the Samuel Goldwyn Studio. After Goldwyn's death, it became a rental studio and was owned for a time by Warner Bros. Today, it is a television facility called the Lot.

By the end of World War I, many independent filmmakers were leasing space from large rental studio facilities, such as the Motion Picture Center Studios, Educational, and Grand National Studios. Later, Nassour opened as a film and television facility on Sunset Boulevard.

FAMOUS PLAYERS FILM CORP., 1915. Located on the southeast corner of Melrose and Bronson Avenues, this studio lot was the West Coast home of Adolph Zukor's Famous Players Company. In the photograph above are, from left to right, Albert Kaufman, an unidentified man, Charlotte Pickford (Mary's mother), Mary Pickford, director/actor Donald Crisp, and director Allan Dwan. Below, Pickford sits on stage during the filming of *A Girl of Yesterday* (1915) while director Allan Dwan (left) and Mary's brother Jack Pickford clown for the cameras in the background.

CLUNE STUDIOS, 1915.
Theatre owner William
H. Clune purchased the
Famous Players lot in
1915 and produced the
film *Ramona* that same
year with Donald Crisp as
director. The photograph
at right looks east towards
the Clune lot from what
is now Bronson Avenue.
Crisp and his cast are
visible at the bottom of
the photograph on the
Ramona sets, which were
located on the west side
of Bronson Avenue.

CLUNE STUDIOS/PARALTA PRODUCTIONS, 1918. The Clune lot served as a rental property for independent film companies. Here, members of three companies of Paralta Productions are assembled together. Among the group are directors George Seitz, Al Green, Reginald Barker, Donald Crisp, Wallace Worsley, and Oscar Apfel and stars J. Warren Kerrigan, Bessie Barriscale, and Agnes Ayers.

CLUNE STUDIOS, 1916; TEC-ART, 1927. Today's Raleigh Studios began life as Fiction, though it became the Famous Players West Coast studio before being acquired by theater owner William H. Clune (above). Clune made two pictures here and then leased the studio out to independent producers. Over the years, many companies have hung out a shingle here, including the Paralta Corp., Douglas Fairbanks Productions, United Artists, Paramount, Prudential, Sherman, Schulberg, California, Producers Studio, and Tec-Art, which is pictured below in 1927. Today, it is Raleigh Studios, a well-known rental lot. Incidentally, it is also the home of coauthor Marc Wanamaker's Bison Archives.

CALIFORNIA STUDIOS, 1958; PRODUCERS STUDIOS, 1979. Today's Raleigh Studios at 5300 Melrose Avenue in Hollywood claims to be one of the longest continually operated studios in the country. One of the reasons for its longevity is how quickly it adapted to the new medium of television. It was here that such long-running shows as *Perry Mason*, *Gunsmoke*, *Have Gun—Will Travel*, and *Superman* were filmed. For a time in the 1950s, Raleigh was called California Studios (above), and in the 1970s, it was known as Producers Studios (below). Commercial developers Raleigh Enterprises, the studio's current owner, purchased the studio in 1979 with the intention of tearing it down to build a Kmart but, seeing the potential in the property, ended up expanding and updating the facilities.

CALIFORNIA STUDIOS, 1943. Star Richard Dix is surrounded by the Victory Girls, a group of starlets fundraising for the war effort, on a visit to California Studios in 1943. Dix began life in Minnesota in 1893 as Ernst Carlton Brimmer and began making films in the silent era before successfully transitioning to sound. He is primarily remembered today for his roles in 1931's Best Picture winner *Cimarron* and the British science fiction film *Transatlantic Tunnel* (1935).

SPACE PATROL, 1952. An episode of the 1950s science fiction show *Space Patrol* is pictured being filmed inside of California Studios. The following April, *Space Patrol* made history by becoming the first television show to have an episode broadcast in 3-D. The show was based around the 30th-century adventures of Commander Buzz Corry and Cadet Happy, played by Ed Kemmer and Lyn Osborn.

BRUNTON STUDIOS, 1919 AND 1923. Paralta Studios, located at 5451 Marathon Avenue, was taken over by Scotsman Robert Brunton, who created Brunton Studios. Brunton ran the lot as a rental property for independent producers, charging a fee for everything from stage space to secretarial assistance. Pictured above is the glass stage where independent companies leased space. Below, the large multi-purpose stage on the left could be split into two stages. The art department and dressing rooms were attached to this building, making it one unit. The view is to the north, and barely visible in the distance is the new (at that time) Hollywood sign.

UNITED STUDIOS, 1923 AND 1926. Due to illness, Robert Brunton was not able to hold on to his new studio for very long. Michael Charles "M.C." Levee bought him out in 1921, renaming the property United Studios. Joseph M. Schenck soon engineered a deal to buy United from Levee while keeping him on as president. After the purchase, Schenck brought his stable of talent west. This included the Talmadge sisters, Constance and Norma (Schenck's wife), and Buster Keaton. After 1926, this lot became the headquarters of Paramount Pictures, which began on Poverty Row in 1913. The above aerial view shows United Studios at the lower half of the frame, and at the top is what is today known as Hollywood Forever Cemetery—the permanent home of several filmmakers who once plied their trade on Poverty Row. Below, Paramount studio heads Adolph Zukor (left) and Jesse L. Lasky survey construction at their new lot in 1926.

PARAMOUNT STUDIOS, 1926. By the mid-1920s, the Famous Players–Lasky lot on Selma Avenue and Vine Street was no longer large enough to adequately handle all of Paramount's West Coast productions. To alleviate the problem, Adolph Zukor and Jesse Lasky purchased the 26-acre United Studios on Marathon Street and embarked on a massive $1-million overhaul of the property. In this photograph, United Studios owner M.C. Levee hands the key to the property to its new owner, Jesse L. Lasky, while others look on. From left to right are Betty Bronson, Lasky, B.P. Schulberg, Hector Turnbull, Levee, Mary Brian, and Milton Hoffman.

GENERAL SERVICE STUDIOS, 1936. General Service Studios (GSS), located on the corner of Santa Monica Boulevard and Las Palmas Avenue, has invited a host of Hollywood's favorite stars through its gates over the past 95 years. It began life in 1919, when John Jasper, Charlie Chaplin's set designer, built three unit stages with offices and dressing rooms attached at what was then known as Hollywood Studios (or Jasper Hollywood Studios). This was the studio home of comic Harold Lloyd for many years. Monogram Pictures was a tenant briefly before moving to its Los Feliz facility. During the 1930s, GSS hosted productions starring the Marx Bros., Mae West, Laurel and Hardy, Carey Grant, and Fred Astaire. In later decades, GSS became the home of several hit television shows. It was here on Stage 2 that *I Love Lucy* filmed its first two seasons, becoming the first West Coast television show to tape on film in front of a live audience. During the 1960s, the lot hosted *The Beverly Hillbillies, The Addams Family, Petticoat Junction, Life With Father, Mr. Ed, Ozzie and Harriet, The George Burns and Gracie Allen Show,* and *Perry Mason.* Today, the lot is known as Hollywood Center Studios.

METROPOLITAN STUDIOS, 1925. Before the former Hollywood Studios at 1040 North Las Palmas Avenue in Hollywood became General Service Studios, it was for a time known as Metropolitan Studios. Producer B.P. Schulberg purchased the 15-acre lot from founder John Jasper in the early 1920s before selling the property to Hollywood pioneer Al Christie in 1925. Christie renamed the lot Metropolitan Studios. It was at Metropolitan that millionaire Howard Hughes entered the film business, pouring much of his family's fortune into films like *Swell Hogan* (unreleased), *Two Arabian Knights* (1927), and *Hell's Angels* (1930), a big-budget World War I aerial war film that featured Jean Harlow's screen debut and claimed the lives of three stunt pilots.

METROPOLITAN STUDIOS, 1925. From its beginning, Hollywood Studios was managed by C.E. Toberman, who owned some of the frontage property bordering Santa Monica Boulevard. When Al Christie bought the studio, Toberman kept the property, forcing Christie to create a new entrance to the lot from off of Las Palmas Avenue (below, as General Service Studio in 1936). Christie went bankrupt in 1933, and General Service was formed to operate the studio and pay back the creditors. The lot became an important rental property, with United Artists and Paramount as two of its more important clients.

MOTION PICTURE CENTER STUDIOS, 1951. Actress Patricia Knight strolls the Motion Picture Center Studios lot at 846 North Cahuenga Boulevard, which began life in 1918 as Backlot No. 3 for Metro Studios. In 1953, Lucille Ball and Desi Arnaz took over the property, making it Desilu-Cahuenga Studios. This was the longtime home of such television hits as *I Love Lucy, The Dick Van Dyke Show, Hogan's Heroes, That Girl, My Favorite Martian,* and *I Spy.*

PATRICIA KNIGHT, 1951. Despite having no formal film training, photogenic actress Patricia Knight appeared in five movies during the 1940s and 1950s, thanks in part to the prompting of her then-husband, Cornel Wilde. Here, Knight enters Poverty Row's Motion Picture Center Studios (today's Red Studios Hollywood) at 846 North Cahuenga Boulevard during filming of 1951's *The Magic Face.*

METRO PICTURES, 1915 AND 1918. Metro Pictures, pictured above, was located at Eleanor Street and Lillian Way in Hollywood near Cahuenga Boulevard. The studio expanded rapidly into the surrounding neighborhoods and eventually had a main lot and three backlots. Below, the Metro studio had a Japanese garden behind an administrative building. Richard Rowland and Louis B. Mayer founded Metro Pictures in 1915, but Mayer left to form Louis B. Mayer Productions two years later. Marcus Loew purchased the studio in 1920. In 1916, the Lone Star Film Company took control of this lot for its star, Charlie Chaplin. Buster Keaton moved in after Chaplin and made some of the greatest comedies of the silent era here. In 1924, Metro, Goldwyn Pictures and Louis B. Mayer Productions were merged together to form Metro-Goldwyn-Mayer (MGM).

UNITED ARTISTS STUDIOS, 1927. This lot at 7200 Santa Monica Boulevard opened as the Jesse D. Hampton Studios in 1918 before becoming the Pickford-Fairbanks Studios in 1922. It became United Artists Studios five years later. In 1938, Samuel Goldwyn purchased the property. For a time, it was known as Warner Hollywood Studios. Today, it is a rental property known simply as the Lot.

SAMUEL GOLDWYN STUDIO, 1937. This studio at the corner of Formosa Avenue and Santa Monica Boulevard was not officially known as the Samuel Goldwyn Studio until 1955, when Goldwyn bought the property from Mary Pickford. But that never stopped Samuel Goldwyn, one of the most successful independent producers in history, from telling everyone it was his studio. Between 1980 and 1999, Warner Bros. owned the property at 7200 Santa Monica Boulevard.

VIDOR VILLAGE, 1921. Director King Vidor enjoyed a six-decade career in Hollywood straddling the silent and talkie eras. A native of Texas, Vidor migrated to Southern California in 1915. Beginning as an extra at Universal, Vidor was soon directing, and by 1920, he had his own small studio at 7250 Santa Monica Boulevard, which he called Vidor Village (above). In 1923, the studio was sold to Sol Lesser and renamed Principal Pictures Studios (below).

EDUCATIONAL STUDIOS, 1925. Earl W. Hammons founded Educational Pictures as a distributing company in 1915. In 1923, Hammons began producing his own series of comedies for Educational release at the Fine Arts Studio in East Hollywood (where D.W. Griffith made *The Birth of a Nation* and *Intolerance*) before purchasing Sol Lesser's Principal Pictures Studios (the former Vidor Village) in 1925, pictured above. Some of the comedy units produced here at this time were Hamilton, Mermaid, Juvenile, Tuxedo, and Cameo. Below, at left, Hamilton Comedies star Lloyd Hamilton and director-general Jack White (in the white cap) are seen on the Educational lot with two unidentified men.

Educational Studios, c. 1925. Educational Studios, at 7250 Santa Monica Boulevard, pictured above and below, originally produced instructional films but soon found comedy shorts more profitable. These films were presented in theaters before the main features and were often the highlight of the evening. Educational featured an impressive array of talent in its shorts, including Al St. John, Lloyd Hamilton, Felix the Cat, Edward Everett Horton, Andy Clyde, Moran and Mack, Ford Sterling, and Harry Langdon. Several stars first appeared on screen in Educational shorts, including Shirley Temple and Roy Rogers. Educational also had production facilities in New York based in the Astoria Studios in Queens where Bob Hope, the Ritz Brothers, Milton Berle, Imogene Coca, and Danny Kaye made their big screen debuts. Disgraced silent comic Roscoe "Fatty" Arbuckle occasionally directed Educational shorts there after losing his acting career to scandal.

GRAND NATIONAL STUDIOS, 1937. Educational Studios' fate was sealed when Twentieth Century–Fox, Educational's distributor, ceased supporting its products. E.W. Hammons, Educational's chief, tried to keep his company afloat by entering the feature film market in 1939 by acquiring Grand National Pictures, which was founded by Edward L. Alperson in 1936. The company was able to lure James Cagney away from Warner Bros. for a time before both Educational and Grand National folded. It was taken over in 1943 by PRC (Producers Releasing Corporation) and later became ZIV Studios, the home of *The Cisco Kid*, *Highway Patrol*, *Bat Masterson*, and *Sea Hunt*. This photograph was taken on the Grand National lot during the filming of *Swing It, Sailor!* (1938), which starred Wallace Ford and Isabell Jewell.

Nassour Studios, 1949. In 1945, the Nassour brothers opened a studio at 5746 Sunset Boulevard, on the southeast corner of Sunset Boulevard and Van Ness Avenue. The studio served as home for the Nassours' own production company and as a rental property for live action and animation. Between 1946 and 1950, the studio hosted productions from Allied Artists–Monogram, Abbott and Costello Productions, Sam Bischoff Productions, Jack Wrather Productions (*The Lone Ranger*), Eagle-Lion, Lippert, and United Artists. In 1950, the studio was sold to KTTV Television and became home to Bob Clampett Productions' hit *Howdy Doody*.

Six

WEST LOS ANGELES'S POVERTY ROWS

Since the beginning of the Southern California film industry, most "Hollywood" movies were created somewhere else. This is especially true of the west side of Los Angeles, where thousands of films were made over the decades, far from the inland Los Angeles district of Hollywood.

One of the first filmmakers to come nearer to the coast was Thomas Ince when the Bison Company relocated to a new site in Santa Monica with Ince as director-general. Ince named his sprawling new digs "Inceville." It was here that William S. Hart made many of his most successful films and later took control of the lot, which he renamed "Hartville."

In 1915, Thomas Ince founded the Triangle/Ince Studios on Washington Boulevard in Culver City, on Los Angeles's west side. Chicago's Essanay Film Company opened a small studio nearby a few months later. Other studios followed, including J. Charles Davis, Pacific, Romayne, and Henry Lehrman.

Culver City was soon home to several major and mini-major studios, including MGM (today's Sony Pictures Studios), Selznick International Studios (where 1939's *Gone With the Wind* was made), and Hal Roach Studios.

While the story of Southern California's film industry is often only glimpsed through the lens of these major and mini-major studios, it is important to remember that a great deal of the coming era's major stars, producers, directors, and technicians first cut their filmmaking teeth at the micro-studios around the corner.

INCEVILLE, 1913. Thomas Ince, "The Father of the Western," began his career with Edison before joining Carl Laemmle's IMP Company as a director in 1910. The following year, Ince joined the New York Motion Picture Company (NYMPC) after learning it was building a new studio in Edendale to make Westerns, his preferred genre. In Edendale, Ince streamlined the moviemaking process, developing what were then the revolutionary concepts of scheduling and budgeting individual scenes and employing the use of shooting scripts. When NYMPC's Keystone unit moved to the former Bison lot in Edendale in 1912, Bison relocated to an 18,000-acre ranch in Santa Ynez Canyon along the Pacific coast, where Ince built a state-of-the-art Western studio that he christened "Inceville." Pictured here in 1913, the Miller Brothers 101 Wild West Show performs for the Inceville staff.

INCEVILLE, MID-1910S. In 1912, the Bison Company, which was owned by the New York Motion Picture Company, was relocated from Edendale to the Santa Monica coast at the intersection of Pacific Coast Highway and Sunset Boulevard. The new studio (above), which was headed up by Thomas Ince, became known as "Inceville." The New York Company then installed its Keystone unit, headed by Mack Sennett, in the old Bison lot. Below, Thomas Ince welcomes Joe Miller of the Miller Brothers 101 Wild West Show and Chief Eagleshirt of the Sioux tribe at Inceville. The Miller company signed with Ince to appear in his Westerns.

HENRY LEHRMAN STUDIO, 1920. Henry Lehrman, one of the true Poverty Row pioneers, was seemingly everywhere during the early years of the Southern Californian film industry. After leaving Sunset Boulevard's Poverty Row behind, Lehrman established his L-KO Comedies unit in Culver City at his new Henry Lehrman Studio, pictured here. The property was later taken over by Fatty Arbuckle for a time before scandal wrecked his career. In 1923, the property, located on Washington Boulevard near National Boulevard, later became part of the Hal Roach Studio.

MASTER PICTURES CORP., 1920. The Master Pictures Corporation, the West Coast production arm of Mastodon films, leased a portion of the Culver City Studio at Exposition Boulevard and Arnaz Avenue to produce *You Know Me, Newlywed,* and the Lester Allen comedies. Master remained here until 1924.

PACIFIC FILM COMPANY, 1922. This tiny Culver City studio at 9147 Venice Boulevard had only one stage and a small New York Street backlot. By 1927, the studio was known as Ambassador Studios. It later became the Bryan Foy Studio and, by 1935, the Sam Katzman Studio. It was later destroyed by fire before becoming a factory.

J. CHARLES DAVIS STUDIO, 1929. The Pacific Film Company originally opened in 1915 as a branch of the Essanay Film Company of Chicago. It later changed hands several times before becoming Ambassador Studios. Producer J. Charles Davis assumed control of the property shortly afterwards and installed sound equipment to make talkies.

ROMAYNE STUDIOS, 1920. The Romayne Superfilm Company Studios, located on the northeast corner of Ince and Washington Boulevards in Culver City, was another of the early West Los Angeles rental studios. Producer Henry Y. Romayne owned Romayne. Warner Bros. produced a two-reel comedy here starring Monty Banks. The lot was not ideal—Jack Warner called it "a dump" in his autobiography. Romayne was not the first motion picture studio in Culver City. Thomas Ince built one here in 1915. MGM (today's Sony Pictures Studios), Selznick International Studios (where 1939's *Gone With the Wind* was made), and Hal Roach Studios soon followed.

HAL E. ROACH STUDIOS, 1922. Hal Roach began as an extra in Hollywood in 1912. Money from an inheritance got him into producing Lonesome Luke films with his friend Harold Lloyd in Edendale and at the Crosby Studios in downtown Los Angeles before moving to 8822 Washington Boulevard in Culver City around 1919. Roach produced hundreds of films here starring Will Rogers, Charley Chase, Harry Langdon, Thelma Todd, ZaSu Pitts, and Patsy Kelly, but his most famous employees were Laurel and Hardy and the Our Gang kids. Changing audience tastes in the 1930s caused him to phase out short films, his staple throughout his career, and he began making full-length features. During World War II, his studio was converted into "Fort Roach," where the Army made 400 instructional and propaganda films. Roach later moved heavily into television production here, with an output of 1,500 hours of programming created in 1951. Roach retired from production in the mid-1950s. In 1984, he was awarded an honorary Academy Award, and he would live to the age of 100, dying in 1992. Roach's 14.5-acre studio, the "Lot of Fun," was torn down in 1961.

LINCOLN MOTION PICTURE COMPANY, 1917. African American brothers George and Noble Johnson founded the Lincoln Motion Picture Company in Omaha, Nebraska, in 1915. They planned to create so-called "race movies," films catering to largely African American audiences that more accurately depicted members of their community, hoping to counteract negative stereotypes found in many mainstream films of the time. By 1916, Lincoln moved west to 1215 Tennessee Street in West Los Angeles. Here, Lincoln produced several films, including *The Realization of a Negro's Ambition* and *Trooper of Company K.* Noble Johnson, a popular character actor, had a long screen career, appearing in several notable titles, including *The Four Horsemen of the Apocalypse* (1921), *The Ten Commandments* (1923), *The Thief of Baghdad* (1924), *The Mummy* (1932), *King Kong* (1933), *Lost Horizon* (1937), and *She Wore a Yellow Ribbon* (1949). Above is a stage from one of Lincoln's productions. To the right is actress Beulah Hall and Lincoln cofounder Noble Johnson.

Seven

OTHER EARLY POVERTY ROW STUDIOS

Throughout the past century, there have been several studios located in the vicinity of downtown Los Angeles, beginning with the very first studios in the region.

The Biograph Company was one of the first to tap into Los Angeles's nearly limitless sunshine, sending D.W. Griffith here on three occasions to set up temporary studios. Its main lot in downtown Los Angeles is today covered by Staples Center, the home of the Los Angeles Lakers.

Also near downtown is the former Bosworth Studio at 201 North Occidental Boulevard, which was created in 1914 by Hobart Bosworth, one of the founders of Paramount Pictures. Bosworth's studio became an annex for Paramount for many years until it was acquired by several independent companies. During the 1960s, it was known as Aldrich Studios. Today, it is a rental lot known as Occidental Studios.

In the early days, some producers, like Colonel Selig and David Horsley, also became zoo owners in order to have a ready supply of exotic animals for their jungle films.

Movie studios went from being shunned by locals in the early days of Hollywood to being highly sought after businesses, with municipalities competing with one another for a slice of the moviemaking pie. Occasionally, this resulted in the actual creation of new cities, like in the case of Universal City and Studio City.

Carl Laemmle first created Universal City in April 1913 on the San Fernando Valley's Universal Oak Crest Ranch. He moved his studio/city to the current Universal City in March 1915. Studio City was developed in 1927 by Al Christie for Mack Sennett as an enticement to move his operations into the mostly empty San Fernando Valley. The former Sennett studio was later purchased by Mascot, which became a part of Republic Studios before being acquired by CBS. In the 1950s and 1960s, this was the home of several hit television shows, including *Leave It To Beaver*, *Gunsmoke*, *Have Gun—Will Travel*, and *Gilligan's Island*. Today, it is known as CBS-Radford Studios.

AMERICAN MUTOSCOPE AND BIOGRAPH COMPANY, 1911. In 1910, the New York–based American Mutoscope and Biograph Company sent director D.W. Griffith and Mary Pickford, its main star, to the West Coast, where they set up three studios during a two-year period. Between trips back east, they created a temporary studio at 312 California Avenue in Santa Monica. They later moved to Grand and Washington Streets in downtown Los Angeles, and in 1911, they settled for a time at 906 Girard Street (now the corner of Pico Boulevard and Georgia Street, pictured above and below). Griffith and his equally legendary cameraman Billy Bitzer worked together at all three of these studios, where they developed new techniques of camera usage and lighting. Griffith and Bitzer later left Biograph and settled in Hollywood in a lot at 4500 Sunset Boulevard. It was here they made the silent epics *The Birth of a Nation* (1915) and *Intolerance* (1916). The old Biograph lot on Girard Street was replaced by the Los Angeles Convention Center and Staples Center, the home of the Los Angeles Lakers, Clippers, Kings, and Sparks.

BOSWORTH-MOROSCO STUDIO, 1929. The above studio at 201 North Occidental Boulevard near downtown Los Angeles first opened in 1915 as the Bosworth Studio, the studio home of Hobart Bosworth. Bosworth later teamed up with Oliver Morosco, and it became the Bosworth-Morosco Studio. Morosco was born Oliver Mitchell in Utah and was later adopted by his boss, showman Walter Morosco. He moved to Los Angeles, where he became a theatrical producer, staging several successful shows in Los Angeles and on Broadway in New York. Bosworth and Morosco were both brought in as initial partners in the merger that created Paramount Pictures. Morosco was later bankrupted by land speculation before being killed by a streetcar in Hollywood in 1945. For a time, the property was known as Paramount-Artcraft and Paramount–Reel Art Studios. During the 1960s, the studio belonged to producer-director Robert Aldrich (below).

ALDRICH STUDIOS, 1968. Producer-director Robert Aldrich purchased the studio at 201 North Occidental Boulevard in 1968. Aldrich, a blue-blooded Easterner, was disinherited by his wealthy parents (his cousin was Nelson Rockefeller) after informing them that he wanted to work in the movies. He apprenticed with Jean Renoir and Charlie Chaplin before directing his first feature in the 1950s. He is remembered today for such notable films as *Kiss Me Deadly* (1955), *Whatever Happened to Baby Jane?* (1962), *Hush . . . Hush, Sweet Charlotte* (1964), *The Flight of the Phoenix* (1965), *The Dirty Dozen* (1967), and *The Longest Yard* (1974). Above, Aldrich shows off architectural plans for his new studio. Below, a line of models celebrates at the opening. The studio exists today as Occidental Studios.

**ROLIN FILM COMPANY, 1914
AND 1918.** Pictured at right in
1914, the Rolin Film Company
was headquartered at the Crosby
Studio, a lot on Court Street
in downtown Los Angeles.
The studio was originally the
Bradbury family mansion on
Bunker Hill before James Crosby,
a former cameraman with Selig,
got control of the property and
opened it up as a rental facility.
Below, Hal Roach's Rolin
Company films at the studio in
1918, when it was known as the
Court Street Studio. Among the
group are Hal Roach (far left),
an unidentified cameraman,
Harold Lloyd (wearing glasses),
Snub Pollard (with mustache),
Bebe Daniels, and director
Henry Lehrman (seated).

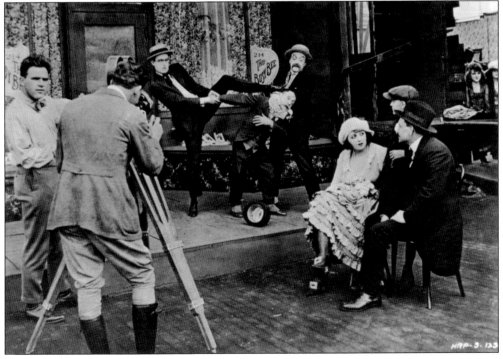

BERNSTEIN STUDIOS, 1917. Studios grew like mushrooms around Southern California during the early decades of the 20th century, and many closed as quickly. The Boyle Heights district, just east of downtown Los Angeles, once had two studios—Majestic/Essaway, where Chaplin worked for a time, and Bernstein Studios, pictured above and below. This company, located at 763 Boyle Avenue, was owned by Isadore Bernstein, who made films that were released by Universal. Bernstein's studio was located on the eight-acre Perry Estate, which was gifted by lumber baron William Perry to his daughter and her husband, the grandparents of actor Robert Stack. Only a handful of films were made here by Bernstein, including *Who Knows?* (1917) with Betty Brice and *Nuts In May* (1917), a film notable for giving Stan Laurel his first starring role.

SELIG STUDIO-ZOO, 1929. In 1911, Colonel Selig purchased land at 3800 Mission Road in East Los Angeles, several miles south of his studio in Edendale. The property in Lincoln Park (then known as Eastlake Park) was used to build a combination studio and zoo, with the animals appearing in jungle movies made on-site when not entertaining the guests. In a 1917 issue of *Moving Picture World*, reporter G.P. Von Harleman wrote, "The Selig Zoo at Eastlake Park is one of the show places of Los Angeles. It covers thirty-two acres of ground and is situated at 3800 Mission Road. Col. Selig has assembled here one of the largest animal collections in the United States. At the entrance to the zoo is an animal sculpture [pictured here] of great beauty. The studio-zoo is of Mission Style with a large patio and well-kept lawn. There are many different animal compounds and an amusement pavilion in the center. The studio part of the zoo is at the rear end of the park. Near the stages are concrete dressing rooms, shops and a camera department."

SELIG STUDIO-ZOO, 1923 AND 1916. Selig was eventually bankrupted by the zoo, which never became the major tourist attraction that he hoped it would be. He died in 1948. Above, a production financed by Louis B. Mayer and directed by John M. Stahl films at the zoo studio in 1923. Mayer based his operations here after Selig left the film production business around 1920. Many famous animals resided at the Selig Zoo, including the first Leo the Lion, who was originally seen at the opening of Goldwyn Pictures. Leo became the mascot for MGM (Metro-Goldwyn-Mayer) in 1924 after Goldwyn Pictures merged with Metro Pictures and Mayer's L.B. Mayer Productions. Below, trucks move equipment behind the scenes in 1916.

BOSTOCK JUNGLE & FILM COMPANY, 1915. David Horsley was yet another producer who bought a zoo, pictured above. Built in 1887, and later known as Chutes Park, it was one of the West Coast's first amusement parks, with attractions, a zoo, a theater, and a baseball stadium that was home to the Los Angeles Angels of the Pacific Coast League. It was located on South Main and Eighteenth Streets near downtown Los Angeles. Horsley, who along with his brother William was one of the film industry's true pioneers, built Hollywood's first studio in 1911 and later became one of the founders of Universal Pictures. He created the five-acre studio at Chute's Park in July 1915 after acquiring the Bostock Zoo animals. When not filming jungle movies, Horsley put on live animal shows for the public. The entire area was abandoned by 1925, and today, like so many of Los Angeles's historical sites, it is a parking lot. Below, notice the gallery of spectators lining seats above the filming—a common practice during the silent era.

E&R JUNGLE FILM COMPANY, 1915. Col. William Selig and David Horsley were not the only early Hollywood producers to have a zoo. J.S. Edwards and John Rounan founded the E&R Jungle Film Company at 1720 North Soto Street in 1914 to serve as a zoo and provide exotic animals for jungle films. This zoo was close to Selig's zoo and was populated by animals collected by Edwards over the course of 30 years. Some of the titles made here include *Children of the Jungle*, *Hunting the Regal Python*, and *Sally the Chimp*. E&R's star chimpanzees, Sally and Napoleon, were soon starring in their own comedy series of 40 one-reelers. *Tarzan of the Apes* (1918), the first film adaptation of the classic Edgar Rice Burroughs character, is believed to have had scenes filmed at E&R.

WHY MASCOT SERIALS ARE SUPREME

MASCOT PICTURES, 1934. Producer Nat Levine founded Mascot Pictures in 1927. Levine began his career as a personal secretary for MGM boss Marcus Loew and is credited with discovering singing cowboy Gene Autry. Mascot kept afloat by producing low-budget B-Westerns and serials, including 1929's *The King of the Kongo*, which was the first talkie serial. Pictured above is the layout of the former studios of Mack Sennett in Studio City that Levine purchased in 1934. The following year, Herbert Yates would integrate several studios, including Mascot, into his new Republic Pictures. Republic made the former Mascot lot its headquarters. Before becoming part of Republic Pictures, Mascot's mascot was this lion sitting atop a globe (below).

REPUBLIC PICTURES, 1935. Herbert J. Yates, the owner of film processing lab Consolidated Film Industries, created Republic Pictures in 1935. Several Poverty Row studios owed Yates's lab money. Facing foreclosure, six of the studios—Monogram Pictures, Majestic Pictures, Liberty Pictures, Chesterfield Pictures, Invincible Pictures, and Mascot Pictures—agreed to merge together under Yates's leadership to create Republic. Over the next 14 years, Republic produced nearly 1,000 films, specializing in Westerns and serials and shepherding the careers of stars Roy Rogers, John Wayne, and Gene Autry along the way. While many of its films were considered B-pictures, Republic occasionally produced a big-budget A-list film, such as the John Wayne–Maureen O'Hara classic *The Quiet Man* (1952). Republic's studios were originally built in 1927 for slapstick comedy producer Mack Sennett and were located at 4024 Radford Street in Studio City, in the (then) sparsely settled San Fernando Valley. After Sennett lost the studio in the early 1930s, it was the home of Mascot Pictures. Mascot, before it folded into Republic, once tried unsuccessfully to get the area around the studio renamed Mascot City.

Eight

FROM POVERTY ROW TO THE BIG TIME

Poverty Row certainly had its share of studios that popped up like prairie dogs and disappeared just as quickly. But it had its success stories as well. For example, take the saga of Poverty Row neighbors Columbia Pictures and Warner Bros.

During World War I, Columbia Pictures began as a small East Coast distribution company known as the CBC (Cohn-Brandt-Cohn) Film Sales Corporation before brothers Harry and Jack Cohn began making their own films under the CBC Productions banner.

Eventually, CBC settled on Sunset Boulevard's Poverty Row and in 1924 changed its name to Columbia Pictures and began purchasing the properties of surrounding studios. Columbia would eventually take over most of the two square blocks between Sunset Boulevard, Gordon Street, Fountain Avenue, and Gower Street.

Columbia's history is very similar to that of its onetime Poverty Row neighbor Warner Bros. The Warners also began as film distributors back East before moving into production during World War I. For years, both Columbia and Warner Bros. rented stage space at the same small studios in the Los Angeles area before both settled on Poverty Row in the early 1920s.

After the success of its early talkie films in the mid-1920s, Warner Bros. moved most of its principle production out of Hollywood to Burbank. The Warner Bros. Sunset Studio at Sunset Boulevard and Van Ness Avenue was sold in the 1940s and changed hands several times. It became a rental studio for television pilots, such as *Gunsmoke*, and the home of Paramount-Sunset Studios and Paramount's KTLA television station. For a time, it was even a bowling alley. Today, it is again a rental property, the Sunset-Bronson Studios.

Columbia left Poverty Row in 1971 to team up with Warner Bros. on its Burbank lot. Columbia moved to Culver City to make its home in the old MGM lot 20 years later. The former Columbia Studio at Gower Street and Sunset Boulevard was abandoned for a time. It too became a rental lot, which is now called the Sunset-Gower Studios. Today, Hudson Capital owns both the Sunset-Bronson and Sunset-Gower Studios.

Desk laboratory of studio, where all equipment is tested for production.

DISC AND SOUND-ON-FILM RECORDING ROOM.

Sound stage, showing mixer platform and microphone junction box.

COLUMBIA STUDIOS

COLUMBIA'S HOLLYWOOD STUDIOS—MOST COMPLETE TALKING PICTURE PLANT IN THE WORLD

Examining room for light spacing, color values and ribbons.

Wax shaving machine removes sound track for new recording.

Vacuum tank and driving motor to draw shavings during making of wax records.

Recording room for wax records.

Main channel at Columbia studios.

COLUMBIA STUDIOS, 1928 AND 1935. Columbia first took root on Poverty Row as CBC (Cohn-Brandt-Cohn) Productions, becoming Columbia Pictures in 1924 after having secured a spot in the studios centered around Sunset Boulevard and Gower Street. Columbia became the "most complete talking picture plant in the world" (left) by making quality films cheaply, eventually purchasing most of the property between Gower and Gordon Streets. The aerial photograph below shows many of the formerly independent studios that eventually came under the Columbia umbrella. This view looks northeast and shows Sunset Boulevard (top), Gower Street (left), Beachwood Drive (middle), and Gordon Street (right). Beachwood Drive was later incorporated into the Columbia lot and closed to public vehicles. The studio remained here until 1971, when it moved to Burbank to share space with former Poverty Row neighbor Warner Bros. Columbia relocated to the former MGM lot in Culver City two decades later.

SUNSET AND GOWER, 1935.
This view across Gower
Street shows the Columbia
administration building that
was once used in the early
1920s by Chester and Grand-
Asher. The center building
was constructed by Columbia
in 1931, and the other
buildings down the block were
built between 1931 and 1935.
Columbia would be housed in
these structures for 50 years
before leaving Poverty Row
for the Burbank Studios lot in
Burbank, which it shared with
Warner Bros. for 20 years.

SUNSET AND GOWER, 1976. At the time of this photograph, Columbia had already moved
to Burbank, partnering with Warner Bros. by creating a new entity on the WB lot called the
Burbank Studios. The former Columbia lot went through various owners and was left vacant
for a time until it became the Sunset-Gower Independent Studios in the early 1970s. Today, it
is again a rental property, the Sunset-Gower Studios. Until recently, this was the home of the
popular series *Dexter*.

WARNER BROS. SUNSET STUDIOS, 1922. In 1920, the Warner brothers founded their first permanent home here at 5842 Sunset Boulevard, a few blocks east of the heart of Poverty Row at Sunset Boulevard and Gower Street. The peripatetic Warners had rented space all around Los Angeles before earning enough to purchase this vacant lot in Hollywood fronted by Sunset Boulevard and bordered by Van Ness and Bronson Avenues. The 10-acre property was owned by a family named Beesemyer, who arranged for the brothers to pay for the $25,000 lot in installments. It was said that the payments were made in bags of gold coins. The name on the side, "Warner Brothers West Coast Studio," was pure bravado since there was no East Coast studio at the time. It did not look like much in 1922, but the lot at 5842 Sunset Boulevard would soon be the place where Rin Tin Tin would first save the day, where Bugs Bunny would nibble his first carrot, and where the voices of the stars on the silver screen would first be heard.

WARNER BROS. SUNSET STUDIOS, 1924. The Warners' new home in Hollywood changed dramatically in a short time. Only two years after occupying a single building on the grounds, it expanded to encompass nearly the entire 10-acre lot. A new multi-columned main studio building now bordered Sunset Boulevard, with Bronson Avenue on the building's right and Van Ness Avenue on the left side of the property. The original studio building (see page 126) did not disappear but was hidden just behind the new administration building. This would be the home of the Warners for much of the 1920s before their foray into sound films earned them enough money to move to Burbank, where they remain to this day. This original studio site, which still exists on Sunset Boulevard near the Hollywood (101) Freeway, was designated a cultural landmark in 1997 and placed in the National Register of Historic Places in 2002.

DISCOVER THOUSANDS OF LOCAL HISTORY BOOKS
FEATURING MILLIONS OF VINTAGE IMAGES

Arcadia Publishing, the leading local history publisher in the United States, is committed to making history accessible and meaningful through publishing books that celebrate and preserve the heritage of America's people and places.

Find more books like this at
www.arcadiapublishing.com

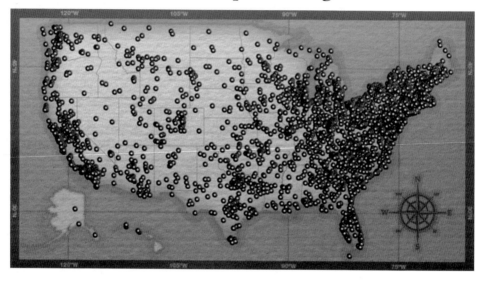

Search for your hometown history, your old stomping grounds, and even your favorite sports team.